I L L U S T R A T E D

NEGOTIATOR'S

G L O S S A R Y

ILLUSTRATED

NEGOTIATOR'S

GLOSSARY

Donald A. Wiesner
Nicholas A. Glaskowsky, Jr.

Illustrations by Joe Bore

Born Negotiator Publishing Group
Coral Gables, Florida

Published by
Born Negotiator Publishing Group, Inc.
5615 Alhambra Circle
Coral Gables, Florida 33146

ISBN 0-9711695-0-0

Table of Contents

List of Terms

What? Me Negotiate? Forget it!

Most of us find ourselves doing some negotiation, such as when we buy a car—a distasteful procedure for nearly everyone—but personal lives don't usually involve a lot of negotiation. However, the business person who lives in a buying and selling environment, the development and improvement of negotiation skills is not an option; it's a necessity. This glossary of terms and concepts is for those who are interested in obtaining a better understanding of the "in" language and behavioral concepts that apply to professional negotiation.

Ok, But Can I Just Get A Quick Fix?

The format serves those who only need a "quick read" as well as bargainers who want more explanation and examples. The quick read material is followed by fuller explanations of the terms or negotiation behavior. The cartoons direct attention to many of the terms as well as sharpening understanding of the terms.

With All Due Modesty I Think I Handle Others Well. Can You Show Me Otherwise?

Six tests are offered the reader. Test One, Temperament, is crafted to permit the reader a self examination of his or her own natural tendencies when exercising negotiation behavior. For some it can be an eye opener. The results could suggest a number of considerations. For example, it might suggest that negotiation is not how you want to make your living. Simply, necessary bargaining mind sets are just too uncomfortable for some people. Or, enlightenment may come from the test results suggesting that a particular attitude about the bargaining game must be overcome, and by gosh, I can do that.

Tests Two through Six challenge your understanding of terms or concepts and allow you to build your negotiation repertoire. They include a review of the monetary increment game, concession behavior and certain negotiation generalizations as well as alerting you to common tactics and some thoughts on international stereotyping.

You can also keep current on the topic of negotiation by checking our web pages from time to time at **www.bornnegotiator.com**

Let the fun begin.

Introduction

This collection of negotiation terms with definitions and illustrations offers professional managers quick understanding of common bargaining theories, practice, and behavior. Much has been written about the theory and practice of negotiation. This outpouring of writing began in the middle 1960's and continues today. These writers come from both the business world and academe. The subject of negotiation is now considered a discipline in many universities. The Harvard Negotiation Project, for example, has brought fresh approaches to the discipline. This glossary, however, provides the day-to-day contractor with a quick view of bargaining behavior.

There is no official authority that defines the various terms and phrases associated with the process of business negotiation. Some are jargon, others are slang, and some are standard words given a special meaning. The terms and phrases presented and defined here reflect the experience of the authors in conducting negotiation exercises in industry seminars. Numbered among these seminar participants were parties engaged in active contracting, including engineers, purchasing personnel and contract managers.

Part One provides a brief definition of each of these negotiation terms and phrases. Part Two expands these definitions and gives examples of the use or application of each.

PART ONE

Brief Descriptions

ACTIVE LISTENING   An "active listener" is one who not only hears what the other party is saying, but also speculates as to the real meaning of what is being said.

AGENDA   An agenda is a list of points introduced at the outset of a negotiation meeting by one of the parties.

AIDE DE MEMOIRE   French expression meaning "an aid to memory." It is a note written to summarize a matter discussed because effective negotiation requires accurate recollection.

ARGUING   The adept negotiator seldom accidentally argues with the other party.

ASPIRATIONS   High goals (aspirations) are necessary in this profession.

AUTHORITY   "Lack of authority" is a ploy sometimes used by negotiators.

BARGAINING CHATTER   At the beginning of a bargaining session the parties usually exchange a variety of comments ranging from the weather to sports, and, if they know each other, perhaps inquiries about spouses or children. The idea is to "break the ice." This is called bargaining chatter.

BATNA   A acronym meaning Best Alternative To a Negotiated Agreement

BODY LANGUAGE   The belief that the thoughts of others are revealed by the movement, or absence thereof, of their hands, eyes, and/or other parts of their bodies.

BOGEY   See "Transference"

BORN NEGOTIATOR   A designation sometimes bestowed on those glib or convincing parties who seem to have natural persuasive abilities.

BOULWARISM   A negotiation approach named after Lemuel R. Boulware, a 1940's General Electric negotiator, who, after extensive fact finding regarding a union settlements, unilaterally determined what was fair in each case and settled on that offer.

BRACKETING   A tactic by which a speaker attempts to establish the other party's upper and lower boundaries.

BREACH OF CONTRACT   A contractual breach is a failure to meet the legal terms of the agreement. Almost all except very simple contracts are breached in some way. While only a "material breach" is important to a contractor, a negotiator can fruitfully use "minor breaches" as trade offs. See "material breach" and "trade off."

CARDS ON THE TABLE   A bargainer says "Let's put our cards on the table!" It is a seeming plea to practice soft bargaining, that is, an exchange of trust between the parties.

CARRYING WORDS   The practice of offering neutral phrases and comments that can be safely said to smooth the road of give and take.

CHERRY PICKING   A tactic whereby one party picks those items which it wants from among those in an almost-settled deal, discarding the rest.

CHINESE AUCTION   A term describing the tactic of stating that one or more other parties are also being considered.

COMPANY POLICY   Some bargainers begin sessions with unfavorable restrictions preceded by the statement "It is our company's policy that. . . ."

COMPROMISE SOLUTION   In negotiation theory this identifies an agreement in which neither party obtained all they wanted. See also "integrative solution."

CONCESSION BEHAVIOR   This describes conduct sometimes called a negotiation dance (which see). Concession behavior is manifested by the exchange of demands in incremental steps in order to reach agreement.

CONFLICT AFTERMATH   This is an academic term for an unhappy negotiator's attempts at revenge after the settlement.

CONFLICT MANAGEMENT   This is an academic sounding name given to the process of negotiation.

COST ANALYSIS   Bargainers, intending to determine price using an objective criterion, sometimes engage in cost analysis.

COST BENEFIT ANALYSIS   Given one's criteria, whether it is better to select A or B is the objective of a cost benefit analysis. When preparing for negotiation this question is answered hypothetically.

COST PLUS CONTRACT   A very tricky type of contract, practiced in some industries by custom. The agreement sets no total fixed price, but rather prescribes that the costs incurred plus the addition of a percentage of the costs for profit be the basis for the total contract price.

CULTIVATION   The practice of successfully wooing a potential contractor by gifts is an ancient negotiation tactic. But today both legal (e.g.,bribery, rebates) and ethical constraints make this less of an option. However, there are other methods of very acceptable cultivation, including treating the other party with courtesy in a variety of ways. See also "Sweetener."

DEADLINE TECHNIQUE   The practice of setting a time or date before which the other negotiator must decide or otherwise act.

DEADLOCK   This term describes the termination of an unsuccessful negotiation where the true intention of the parties was to reach an agreement.

DEFERENCE   In team negotiations the activist is not always the boss. The careful opponent looks for subtle signs of deference one team member exhibits toward another during the session.

DICKERING   A slang name given to an exchange of bids. Sometimes this dialogue is called "haggling."

DOODLING   A gesture in "body language" (which see). It is the writing of unidentifiable drawings on a piece of paper.

DOORKNOB PRICE   See final offer.

ESCALATION   Conduct in which one party, earlier seemingly in agreement, has now changed his or her mind and makes a higher demand on the other.

ESTIMATING WANTS   Parties naturally would like to determine what the other side intends or wants.

ETHICAL CONTRACT   A contract is ethical where both sides are free and conscious of the implications of their acts and neither party has used fraud, power, passion or ignorance to bring about an agreement which otherwise would have been rejected.

EXCITABILITY   The nervous, fast speaking, negotiator is not necessarily an unsuccessful one.

EXPERTS   While there are instances where specialized knowledge or information is needed, skilled negotiators will not be overly impressed by the other side's "experts."

EXPECTED PRICE   When a party informs the other side of "the expected price" for a prospective deal, a tactic is being employed. It is a method used to establish premises favorable to the speaker.

EXPLANATION OF FAILURE   Helping the other party to explain to his or her boss why a negotiation failed can build good will and improve the possibility of future business.

EYE CONTACT   The use of eyes in negotiation, i.e., strongly eyeballing another, is usually perceived by the "target" as being a highly competitive tactic.

EYEGLASSES ON TABLE   A gesture in "body language" (which see). Removing one's eyeglasses during a bargaining session may be taken to suggest some resistance on the part of the actor toward the course of negotiation.

FACE SAVING   The competitive nature of bargaining can result in bad feelings and embarrassment. Experienced negotiators anticipate providing a face saving opportunity for the other side. A supply of trade off items (which see) provides a handy repair kit.

FAIR CONTRACT A term frequently used in contracting although its character is elusive. While dictionaries use such synonyms as "just" and "equitable," the criteria for measuring a contract's terms as just or equitable are not provided.

FINAL OFFER A tactical thrust considered to be useful either only after careful consideration, or where it reflects the truth. It is sometimes called the "doorknob" price."

FIRM OFFER This term is used in several contexts. The speaker may be making an attempt to emphasize the seriousness of his intent, or may have (unintentionally) committed himself legally under the Uniform Commercial Code

FIRST OFFER In negotiation the first offer is rarely the final offer. It simply starts the process. Business negotiations often parallel the military axiom that no battle plan survives the first contact with the enemy.

FIVE PERCENT RULE This is a theory holding that one need be only a small degree better than average in negotiations to be generally successful.

FLINCH An obvious body language reaction to a statement delivered by the other party.

FOLDED ARMS A gesture in "body language" (which see). It is thought to express a defensive position in a bargaining session.

FORWARD MOVEMENT A gesture in "body language" (which see). It is thought to suggest that the party moving toward the other, as in a table negotiation session, is in the process of attempting to agree.

FREEBIES Extras extracted by a party through "nibbling" (which see) after the deal has been made, usually obtained by an aggressive bargainer.

GAME PLAYING Much bargaining behavior looks game-like because of the use of moves and countermoves by the parties.

GENERALIZATION   Adept bargainers have available, as part of their arsenal, a set of generalizations about their company or a position.

GOALS   Setting negotiation goals (price or other terms) must take into account the reality of the negotiation process and the actual business circumstances.

GOOD COP BAD COP   The practice of a negotiating team assigning different roles to its members.

HARD BARGAINING   Negotiation conduct in which a party consciously or unconsciously acts in an adversarial manner in which trust in the other and openness is missing. See also "soft bargaining."

HIERARCHY   In team negotiations the identity of the real decision maker may be disguised.

HIGH INITIAL DEMANDS   A bargaining tactic by which one party initially attempts to produce diminished expectations on the other side.

HIGH PROBABILITY   A term applied to an expectation of success in an upcoming negotiation.

HILLS TO DIE ON   Every decision-maker faces the sort of question expressed by that anonymous Marine who asked, "Is this the hill you want to die on?" Strongly defending a nonessential point may derail a negotiation.

IMPOSSIBLE OFFERS   The practice of stating a proposition that one expects will be rejected out of hand. This is used by negotiators for a variety of purposes.

INDUSTRY PRICING   In the preparation stage of negotiation, the discovery of patterns of industry pricing may permit the bargainer to identify the zone within which the price will likely be negotiated.

INSIDE INFORMATION   In a negotiation setting this term describes a party's secret knowledge of the weaknesses of the other party's position.

INTEGRATIVE SOLUTION   An agreement in which both parties reconcile their interests and settle on a joint benefit. Such a conclusion differs from an agreement in which both parties cede part of their goals by a compromise.

LAST OFFER BEST OFFER   A technique (LOBO) that uses a third party, a mediator, who studies the written offers of each side, tries to get agreement and failing that, makes a selection.

LAWYER NEGOTIATORS   Despite the reality that much conflict requires the services of lawyers, their role in the bargaining process is ill defined.

LECTURERS   A style of presentation used by some negotiators that exhibits an assertive approach.

LEGAL WORDS   Until the parties have reached final agreement, words or phrases that have concrete legal meaning should be used very cautiously.

LEGITIMACY   In negotiations this term has been used to describe a form of perceived power. A company "form contract," a sign announcing a company policy, or an statement of company policy, are examples of attempts to establish the legitimacy of a position taken by the bargainer.

LETTER OF INTENT   A document that appears to set up a contract without it being a binding one. There is no official legal definition of this term.

LEVEL OF ASPIRATION   The level the negotiator has set below (or above) which it would quickly contract with the other. It is part of one's "utility schedule" (which see).

LIMITED MENU   Proposing a select group of options or possibilities narrows the negotiation discussion, as does setting an agenda, (which see). A technique appropriate when there are touchy issues one wishes to avoid.

LINKAGE   The practice of tying one aspect of a proposal to another.

LIST PRICE   Experienced negotiators treat "list price,"" as a tactical ploy, hardly more than bargaining chatter irrelevant to the pending transaction.

Long Term Relationships   Repetitive contracting with another saves negotiating effort, builds trust, and can provide great savings, but it carries some risks.

Lowballing   An offer of an unexpected very favorable term in a bargain. Such a proffer is carefully evaluated by all but the naive.

Low Probability   A term applied to an expectation of limited or poor success in an upcoming negotiation.

Lying   A lie is a statement made to another which, when properly interpreted by the recipient, is known by the speaker to be untrue.

Machiavellians   A negotiator who has confidence in his or her ability to influence others is said to possess the trait attributed by the Italian renaissance court observer Machiavelli to the Italian princes whose reputation for manipulating others is legendary.

Major Points   A bargaining session tends to deal with a number of points and it is common for parties to disguise their greater concerns.

Make Or Buy   The phrase means what it says: should the company make the item (or provide the service) or seek an outside source?

Maneuver   The term "maneuver" is sometimes a synonym for "tactic."

Market   The term "market" or "market price" is a fuzzy term from a practical point of view. The exceptions are true market prices, such as those set on commodity exchanges.

Matter Of Fact   "It's a matter of fact that. . . ." This rather presumptive and fatuous statement is frequently delivered by speakers who should know better. The skilled bargainer uses it sparingly if at all, and rarely acknowledges its worth when spoken by others.

Maximize Profits In negotiations a firm's instruction to its agents to maximize profits is often given and it is believed to be better practical advice than a direction to minimize losses (which see).

Minimize Loses A frequent instruction to company agents is to minimize losses. This is likely to be of questionable value.

Minor Breach It is difficult for a contractor to live up to every term in all but simple contracts. The injured negotiator can use minor breaches as "currency" for other concessions.

Missing Element This term describes behavior similar to the "missing man maneuver" tactic (which see). The missing element can be any needed to close the deal. Experienced negotiators can "smell" this situation and may choose to respond strongly to it.

Missing Man Maneuver Similar to the Missing Element Maneuver, the person whose presence, approval, signature or other manifestation is necessary to seal the deal is absent from the negotiation.

Mock Negotiations Mock negotiation sessions are pretend negotiation exercises. Properly conducted, mock negotiations can be surprisingly realistic.

Monetary Increment Game The pattern in which concession behavior is practiced. It is believed that the distance or spread between sequential offers or proposals affects the expectations and thus future behavior of the other party.

Monkey On Back See transference.

Multiple Choice Questions The practice of presenting multiple options, thus giving the other party a "choice," avoids the yes-or-no response problem.

Negative Qualities Recitation of negative qualities in the other party's product, service, or position is a tactic through which the user attempts to lower the expectations of the other party.

NEGOTIABLE CONTRACTS   In some industries 90% of the contracts are reached without any significant negotiation. The remainder is subject to determining whether the benefits possible from extended negotiations are worth the time, effort and expense spent in the pursuit of better terms than those first offered.

NEGOTIATION DANCE   A name given to the movement of changing positions between the parties.

NEGOTIATION "EXPERTS"   Three groups have contributed to negotiation lore, theory and practice. Popular writers, academics, and seminar leaders form this group of "experts."

NEGOTIATION GOALS   The advanced setting of negotiation goals is a nearly universal practice of experienced negotiators.

NIBBLING   A tactic by which one party attempts to gain additional concessions, usually of a minor nature, after the deal has seemingly been reached. See also "freebies."

NONNEGOTIABLE ITEMS   An early stand taken or statement made in bargaining for the purpose of establishing favorable premises.

OBJECTIVE CRITERIA   Objective standards are being invoked when bargainers suggest that verifiable data be used in the session.

OBSTINACY   While inflexibility causes deadlocks more often than conciliatory tones, its practitioners tend to be more successful than those practicing the latter.

OPEN PRICE   A contractual term by which the parties agree to set the price later, or the price will be set by the "market." This is common in some businesses and in regard to certain products or services. The Uniform Commercial Code provides rules governing this, thus protecting the parties, mostly the payer, from above-market prices.

Opening Statements   An opening statement may range from a simple pleasantry to a calculated employment of a tactic (which see).

Opportunity Cost   A favorite phrase of economists, it simply means that by doing one thing you forego what you could have gained by doing something else with the same resources.

Options   A negotiator needs options to bargain effectively, but sometimes it appears that there aren't any. Such situations challenge the negotiator to use knowledge and imagination to create options not previously considered. See "trade off" hints.

Partners Theory   A form of bargaining in which the parties either speak or think that they are negotiating as if they were partners, so to speak. Partners is a word that should be avoided as it is legally unwise to use the word "partner" in any context or situation other than an actual legal relationship. See "soft bargaining," and "questionable legal words."

Patience   The quality of patience is one of the most valuable talents a negotiator can possess.

Patters And Nudgers   According to body language lore, parties who pat or nudge another display their superior feeling about power over the other.

Performance Specification   A contract term describing the level or manner in which a product or service is promised to perform. It does not technically describe the product or service itself. See "technical specification."

Personalization   This is a tactic in which one's personal problems are incorporated into the negotiation, with a plea for help from the others. This behavior, an emotional appeal, while commonly practiced, is ethically questionable.

Personal Pleas   See Personalization.

PERSUASIVE PERSONALITY   Parties who believe they have the ability to influence others tend to perform better than those lacking such belief.

POSITIONAL BARGAINING   A hard-bargaining term identifying negotiation behavior which exhibits initial extreme positions on each side.

POSTURING   Taking insincere bargaining positions.

POWER, IMPRESSION OF   Even though the elements of power are illusive, it appears, sadly, that many negotiators tend to overestimate the other's clout.

PRECEDENT   Urging approval of terms based on past agreements, or on industry practice.

PREMISES   In negotiation skilled parties attempt to establish premises, either expressly or by implication.

PREPARATION   The perennial formless advice given to parties who have been instructed to negotiate: prepare. The concept is important but frequently the skill to carry out such a task is lacking.

PRICE INCREASES   Announcing possible price increases is a common tactic for softening up the customer.

PRINCIPLED NEGOTIATION   A negotiation theory that argues there is an alternative to either hard or soft bargaining.

PROBLEM SOLVING   Negotiation conduct in which a party practices an open position, one in which trust in the other and openness about one's needs, concerns and difficulties is present. This is a form of "soft bargaining," (which see).

PUFFING   "Bragging" statements, seemingly of fact, but legally considered non actionable.

PUT DOWNS   The use of expressions to decrease expectations or otherwise persuade. There are degrees of aggressiveness both as to content and intent.

QUESTIONS   A means for encouraging further negotiation by give and take.

Quick Negotiations   Quick settlements tend to produce extreme outcomes, leaving a big winner and a big loser.

Quick Quote   Asking for a quick noncommittal figure is a tactic used by the party requesting it.

Real Estate Contract   Real estate, realty, is a space on earth and those things the law considers permanently attached to it.

Real Reason   Finding the real reason for the other party's position is an elusive objective.

Reservation Price   This is the "bottom line" in a negotiator's authority or intentions. See "resistance point."

Resistance Point   The point in a term which the negotiator has set below (or above) which it will not contract and is resigned to deadlock.

Restating Positions   Through restatement, making the other party's position more explicit.

Restricted Authority   The claim by a negotiator that agreement on certain proposed terms would exceed his authority. Also called the "limited authority" tactic.

Risk Taking   Successful negotiators are risk takers.

Role Playing   A common teaching technique used in seminars for negotiators.

Satisfactory Negotiation   The tendency for negotiators to initially be satisfied that they have performed well in a completed negotiation.

Secret Information   Secretly knowing the other party's weakness(es) with respect to an upcoming negotiation.

Seller's Cost   Sessions often include dialogue concerning the seller's "cost" of an item or service.

Service Contract   A contract promising something other than a tangible product or real estate. The distinction is important, particularly in regard to the legal rules governing the formation and enforcement of such contracts. Examples include promises regarding employment and construction. See also Uniform Commercial Code, Sales, and Real Estate Contracts.

Silence   Silence is sometimes used as a tactic.

Single Source   A negotiation mind-set causing the bargainer to believe that only the other party can provide for its needs.

Situational Power   The perception that circumstances have placed a negotiator in a particularly favorable or difficult bargaining position.

Slips Of The Tongue   Verbal missteps occurring in a bargaining situation.

Soft Bargaining   A negotiation approach which purports to include trust, openness and cooperation between the parties. Sometimes called "problem solving technique," "I win you win," "partner's theory" or "the equitable collaborative method."

Speech Patterns   Speech patterns include vocabulary, tone of expression, cadence and emphasis.

Split The Difference   Offering, after many proposals and counter proposals, a 50-50 split of the remaining difference.

Standard Form Or Clause   The word "standard" is frequently used in bargaining chatter, but the only "official" forms or clauses are those prescribed by law.

Stereotypes   A negotiation stereotype is a generalization about both behavior and people, a neutral term.

Straddling A Chair   A gesture in "body language" (which see). This unusual use of a chair is generally interpreted as a domineering act during a bargaining session.

Substitute Performance   Offering or doing an unagreed act that may in essence comply with the contract terms despite its failure to literally satisfy such terms. A post contract negotiation maneuver.

SWEETENER   A concession offered to induce agreement or movement at the bargaining table.

TACTICS   Tactical conduct employed to secure the objectives set by negotiation strategy.

TAKE IT OR LEAVE IT   A risky technique intended to bring closure to a negotiation by issuance of an ultimatum.

TEAM PLAYING   Having more than one negotiator on a side is common in certain situations and firms.

TELEPHONE NEGOTIATIONS   A risky form of negotiation.

THROWAWAYS   A word describing items or terms one is willing to concede to the other side.

TIME INVESTMENT THEORY   This phrase describes the conduct of some bargainers who, because they have invested a lot of time in a negotiation, persist in trying to close a deal.

TIMING   Timing is almost as important to negotiators as it is to stand-up comedians. Being able to determine at what moment to pursue a point or engage a tactic in negotiations is a valuable skill.

TRADE OFF PREPARATION   In the planning stage each party classifies what terms are essential (a minus), what the company could live with (neutral) and what it could give away (a plus).

TRADE OFFS   The saying goes: "Don't give anything away; get something for something."

TRANSFERENCE   This clever and common tactic is also known as "monkey on the back," "bogey," and by several other names. In effect, one negotiator attempts to transfer his problem to the other by asking for help, or a solution to his problem.

TYPE A CONFLICT   A dispute where the negotiators have the power to reach a satisfactory settlement of differences.

TYPE A PROBLEM   Stated by Edward Levin in *Negotiating Tactics: Bargaining Your Way To Winning (1980)*, a Type A problem is one that is manageable with a known reachable goal that may be pursued, as opposed to a Type B Problem where the problem is veiled; the stated issue is not the real issue.

Type A "Stuff"   Usually interpreted in negotiation situations as describing conduct as contrasted with Type B conduct. In this context Type A persons are defined as aggressive or anxious. See Type B "stuff."

Type B Behavior   The behavior of a low-key bargainer, who in voice and mannerisms displays restraint in movement and language employed. Sometimes this is considered non-confrontational, yet it can hide a hard bargaining approach. See Type A Behavior.

Type B Conflict   A dispute in which the stated issue is not the real issue. Considered difficult to settle unless the real issue can be brought out in the open.

Umbrella Issues   When a negotiator has a hidden agenda this phrase describes the unexpressed ("hidden under an umbrella") issues that make up the hidden agenda.

Uniform Commercial Code   All 50 states have adopted a body of legal rules called by this name. While not all states have enacted identical provisions, generally there is considerable uniformity particularly in Article 2 (sales of goods). Negotiators need some knowledge of the Code (UCC) particularly in regard to transaction in goods, i.e., tangible moveable items such as cotton, machines and the like. Oral promises and one sided written forms can be quickly deployed to form a binding contract with the unwary.

Unintended Slips   See Slips of the Tongue.

Utility Schedule   A term used in negotiation theory to describe the spread between one's aspirations and resistance point regarding agreement.

VENUE GAMES   There is a school of thought holding that advantages accrue to a bargainer when the meeting is on his home ground.

WEAK POSITION   The common fear that one's position is weaker than the other side's.

WHAT IF   A "what if . . ." statement offered as an attempt to restart discussion by posing a possible concession.

YESSABLE QUESTIONS   The practice of asking questions that suggest positive responses. (See also Multiple Choice Questions).

ZERO DEFECTS   A negotiation ploy using this term to suggest very high product quality offerings.

PART TWO

Definitions and Examples

Active Listening

One of the most valuable skills that a negotiator can develop is the ability to be an active listener. Active listening consists of, first, listening carefully to what the other party is saying, and second, how he or she is saying it. The task then becomes one of interpreting the meaning of the words one is hearing as well as any gestures the other is using. Active listening is difficult. It calls for disciplined concentration, and for most of us it has to be a learned technique.

EXAMPLE   *"Yes, we have been buying our material from several other companies but we do like to look around for new suppliers as it is always wise to know what the market is and find even better relationships." What is "heard" by an active listener? The statement itself is a banal generality which really says nothing. So, why are they looking at us? Is their credit bad? Is the quality or delivery of their current suppliers poor? Is a supplier factory about to go on strike? Have they been "stiffing" their suppliers who now are practically refusing to sell to them? Probing is in order, and may be more productive if the listener has done some homework on this firm prior to meeting with them.*

Agenda

A proffered written or spoken agenda is premise setter. A selection of what topics are to be discussed permits the agenda setter to attempt to exclude items that she considers unfavorable for her side to consider. When a premise comes on the scene early it can be hard to dislodge it later. An agenda offered by the other side is viewed by a skilled negotiator as being like something slithering toward you through the grass.

EXAMPLE   *"Let me be frank. We're meeting today to find out whether we would "fit" with you if we make a deal. So, we want to see if these three matters of concern to us will receive a sympathetic reception from you all." Putting only their concerns on the table may significantly affect the negotiating environment, particularly if their "three matters of concern" just happen not to include any concerns you may have. You need to respond in some fashion. A reasonably effective counter tactic is to have an agenda of your own in reserve which you can pull out*

and immediately put on the table. If that is done, one party or the other may decide to say, "Okay, that's enough of this, let's cut the nonsense and start talking about what we're here for."

Aide De Memoire

In addition to being of practical use for both legal and psychological purposes, note taking during, or where not appropriate, shortly after a session, sharpens the writer's insight into the negotiation process. Writing forces the mind to focus on critical elements of bargaining significance as well as being an excellent exercise for developing better listening skills. Telephone negotiations absolutely demand such note taking.

EXAMPLE   Notes of phone conversation with Sam Denton of Chapman Industries at 3:25 pm on 8/14. Sam said,.*"Yes, we might be willing to consider ordering 5000 KBR valves at 22% off your list price provided Sally amends her demand that we return the shipping pallets to your plant at our expense, and we would also want you to supply enough spare gaskets."* I said, *"I'll get back to you."* Sam Denton's statement, as well as your reply, should be noted exactly. If his statement gives you what you want, or much of it, you could use it to initiate an offer to him when next you negotiate, whether that is five minutes or five days later.

Arguing

It is common practice for a person to raise an objection or state some concern regarding a contracting point for the purpose of showing resistance. Yet, a strong rebuttal may merely embarrass the speaker who would rather have the objection stand and even be somewhat appreciated. An argumentative manner may show strength of spirit, but it carries considerable psychological negatives in a negotiation setting. Unfortunately, some bargainers don't realize that their manner of speech or gestures may cause unnecessary conflicts with others. Usually, a simple polite response can diffuse the situation. Such approaches are more fruitful to favorable movement than many other common responses to resistance, such as the aggressive "why" question.

EXAMPLE   *One bargainer could not understand why his—to him—simple questions seemed to send such negative vibrations. He would ask the other party, "Now why would you want to do it that way?" A question such as that is frequently (and correctly) "heard" this way: "What an idiot you are, surely you can see that what you propose is stupid." The speaker, either consciously or unconsciously, wants an argument, and even though he may be correct, his "why" question is not productive behavior. Instead of making a challenging, argumentative statement, a better approach is to be diplomatic, saying something like, "That's interesting. I'd appreciate it if you'd give me a little more of your reasoning for your position on this point."*

Aspirations

Management usually sets high goals with respect to price, quality, delivery, or other terms. The negotiator must sign on to these objectives, for without confidence that high aspirations can be achieved the actor is lacking one of the most important emotional drives fueling a successful transaction. Persons who will be risk averse by reason of the assignment ("You must make a deal!"), or due to their natural tendencies, should not be sent to contract in tough situations.

EXAMPLE   *Barlow was sent to negotiate for an amended lease on a*
warehouse that was no longer needed. Her boss told her
she should try to get the lease terminated, or at least
shortened substantially, but in no event antagonize the
landlord because of the status of other leases with that
party. What aspirations should Barlow entertain? The
negotiation will reveal Barlow's personal attitude toward
risk taking as well as her negotiating skills. The instruc-
tions from her boss are a classic example of the type of
conflicting requirements often laid on someone sent out
to do battle for the firm. But, that's life. She should aspire
to get the lease terminated while maintaining good rela-
tions with the landlord. Any lower aspirations will
reduce her chances of success.

Authority

The doctrines of implied authority and apparent authority
(authority by estoppel) make it difficult for a company to later
argue that a party sent out to "deal" in some way in a business
matter did not have authority to contract. When an "agent" is
placed in a position to bargain without clear warning to the third
party that no authority exists, the law views this as power to bind
within the scope of circumstances. From a bargaining, not necessarily legal, view, all authority is somewhat limited, but the
other party, the law calls the third party, can reasonably demand
that the talks be meaningful.

EXAMPLE   *An oil company had express language in its purchas-*
ing manual that only the members of the purchasing
department could contract. One of the firm's petroleum
engineers was invited to lunch by an equipment sup-
plier. Acceptance of the invitation was not against
company policy. The engineer explained the problem
his field force was having with certain special tools.

The supplier stated that if his firm got a three-year equipment maintenance commitment for the south district the engineer was assured that all field personnel would be trained in the use of the special tools, free of charge. The engineer said, "that's a deal" and initialed the terms on a luncheon napkin prepared by the supplier. If the engineer appeared to a reasonable party, here the supplier, to have legal authority, a court could find such authority either under the doctrine of implied authority or apparent authority. Apparent authority is found by courts in those instances in which one has no authority but has been allowed to be in a position to give such impression to others under the circumstances.

Bargaining Chatter

Most of us have a selection of carry phrases or words for particular situations. Cocktail party talk, for example, is different from the type of general remarks we frequently make at committee meetings. Bargainers also indulge in this practice. Simply, programmed responses help a negotiator's brain play catch-up with the action and mentally assimilate information and formulate strategy during the dickering stage. One party responds to the other by replying with a "carrying phrase." These "package" responses or questions are one way to ensure safe passage and to encourage more dialogue. Because silence during a session is not always helpful to both sides, "safe" comments can fill the void.

EXAMPLE   *How often have you heard expressions like these? "Let's sharpen our pencil on that." "I'm having trouble with that." "That's like comparing apples to oranges." "If you think I'm tough you should meet my boss." "That makes the margins too high." "Maybe you are too big for us."*

"To be honest with you, we're looking at several sources."
"You're talking a one-time deal with long-term concessions."

BATNA

What writers (Fisher, Ury & Patton) call the "best alternative to a negotiated agreement" (BATNA) is the resistance point beyond which the negotiator will not go under any expected circumstances. It is called the "best alternative" because it is what (price or other term) the negotiator can be forced to accept due to the relative strength of the negotiating parties. In other words, he or she can't do any better; it is the best that can be achieved, as bad as it may be. It is literally the best alternative to a negotiated agreement because no "agreement" better than the resistance point could be negotiated. One should note that information revealed during negotiations can change a resistance point in either direction.

EXAMPLE   *Johnson's resistance point is to get at least $45 a unit for an expected order of 2,000 units, and his initial price is $49. Larkin, representing the buyer, makes a counteroffer of $43. Larkin knows Johnson's firm is trying to break into the market with a high-quality product but has yet to land its first customer. The negotiation goes slowly, but eventually Johnson drops the price to $47 and Larkin offers $44. After more discussion Larkin offers $45, saying "If you want to get into the market, you have to accept this offer for two reasons. First, I won't go any higher and, second, the other firms are waiting to see if we buy from you because they trust our judgment. If we don't buy from you it's a good bet the other firms won't either." If Johnson's firm wants to get into the market it has no alternative but to sell at its resistance point of $45, a BATNA.*

Body Language

Considerable attention has been paid to the proposition that body movements and mannerisms reveal intent. The proposition is debatable. Adept negotiators tend to be competent actors when it comes to showing intention. They easily control their gestures and mannerisms. However, less talented negotiators may indeed reveal intent. For them, mannerisms or body movements, such as doodling or rapid eye movement, may be assumed to indicate a probability of boredom or stress, respectively. Other observable behavior includes pursing of lips (ire), shrugging shoulders (indifference), clenching fists (belligerence) etc . . . The problem is deciding whether the observed body language has really given you a useful clue or, alternatively, is either a shrewd attempt to mislead or simply irrelevant. Some say looking for consistency between verbal and nonverbal communications will help, but others say "keep it simple and just go with the words" unless there is very good reason to believe contradictory body language.

EXAMPLE   *Alex was the younger member of a two-person negotiating team and his partner, Wesley, took the lead in the discussions with the other side which involved fairly complex financial calculations. Alex appeared to be paying limited attention, and had been creating lots of complex doodles on his notepad. Barnes, the chief negotiator for the other side, summarized their offer and asked Wesley for his response. Wesley turned to Alex, asking for his opinion. Barnes turned to hide a smile as he figured that by now Alex hadn't a clue. Alex looked up, cocked his head at Barnes, and proceeded to deliver an incisive and deadly accurate analysis of the errors in Barnes' financial presentation. Alex followed this with a counteroffer containing error-free financial calculations.*

Bogey   See "Transference"

Born Negotiator

Because the successful practice of persuading others seems inherited in some individuals they are called "natural" or "born" negotiators. Yet, the varied capabilities required to perform as an expert bargainer are mostly learned. Patience, the ability to "hear" what another is saying or not saying, and play acting maneuvers one must practice need to be coupled with certain approaches to life. Among these are the presence of an adventuresome and optimistic spirit.

EXAMPLE   *Torrance, a young business school graduate, was*
               employed as a trainee in the purchasing department of
               Leavell Industries, a large manufacturing firm. After
               his training period he became an assistant purchasing
               agent and was included as a junior member on the
               department negotiating teams. Torrance was intelli-
               gent, ambitious, and hard working. During the next
               four years his bosses approved his requests to attend
               purchasing seminars, including several on negotiation.
               He carefully observed and learned from the successful
               (and unsuccessful) conduct of the senior purchasing
               team members as well as negotiators of other compa-
               nies. At the end of five years he was promoted to assis-
               tant purchasing manager. He was a very successful
               negotiator and was respected by the sales reps he dealt
               with, especially since he made little use of the ploys used
               by many others. His contemporaries in the department
               often called him a born negotiator. The purchasing
               manager, however, did not subscribe to that view. His
               close observation of Torrance over five years told him
               that Torrance was not a born negotiator. He was a
               made negotiator.

Boulwarism

Anyone watching a typical negotiation has probably entertained
the view that there seems to be a considerable waste of time
practiced by both parties. Boulwarism was so named after a
General Electric company negotiator who attempted to circum-
vent this wasteful practice. He was reported as having carefully
studied both sides of the issues between GE and the union. He
then made a "one and final" offer which he believed took into
full account the financial realities of the company-union dispute. It didn't work, and Boulware had his name forever

attached to attempts to avoid the wasteful and aggravating efforts of the give and take and haggling and dickering of negotiation. Such good intentions have been generally ineffective as they disregard human nature which seems to demand a time-consuming exercise in settling disputes.

EXAMPLE *"Look, we are busy people. I've studied the situation thoroughly, as I'm sure you have. I hate dickering, it's unprofessional and shows a lack of class, forcing us to make ridiculous statements that we know we don't mean and you don't believe. So let's cut to the chase. This is my best and only offer. This is how I see it. Okay?" The offer may in fact be "right on," but for a variety of cultural, psychological, and social reasons, the dickering and haggling must proceed.*

Bracketing

Some negotiators, wishing.to be considered "informed," pretend to have knowledge of a particular event, skill, or a person by making cautious guesses about the unknown so as to maintain the pretense. When practiced by a bargainer the effort is

known as bracketing. Here, the speaker attempts to set a favorable premise by acting as if the speaker knows things about the other's business or the industry. It is a tactic whereby the speaker hopes the other party will believe the speaker already has a lot of information, reducing, hopefully the high expectations of the other. Its use may be effective when a speaker hopes to prevent a high initial price from being offered. The "bracket" refers to the upper and lower limits of the price range. Any quantitative term, however, is fair game for the bracketer.

EXAMPLE   *"Now Charlie we're not going to have trouble getting a 3-year warranty on this item, are we? After all, we like your product but you know this is a close industry, people talk, and things do go wrong at times." The inference here is Charlie's product has been getting some bad product press. Maybe the speaker has only suspected as much, but wants to make sure he or she does not get a 1-year warranty offer. The bracketer must have an answer ready should specifics of the "rumor" be demanded.*

Breach Of Contract

Simple contracts exist and they rarely require negotiations. But, when parties spend time and effort crafting a more complicated agreement, many terms are included and some may have a curious life . . . and death. First, the phrasing of a term in relation to expectation may be flawed. Further, some terms may have been included that one or both sides had not really wanted, but considered them irrelevant as they would not come into play. Comes time for performance, some terms become oppressive and one side accidently or deliberately stumbles in some degree. Accordingly, breaches occur. The question then becomes what to do about a breach. Negotiate some additional consideration? Insist on performance? Forget it if it isn't hurtful? Accept it and say "you owe us one." The flexible negotiator knows that some terms may not be met and will be prepared to deal with such circumstances.

EXAMPLE *"But you know that the whole point of the contract was that we were entitled to [fill in the blank]." "Charlene, I don't find that provision or anything like it in any of the contract terms. Clearly, your company agreed to do what we insist you do. The type of a contingency you're raising was never discussed." Both parties may be "correct," but not legally. The complainer may have intentionally failed to bring up the "point" in the negotiation sessions because either it might kill the deal or cost too much. So, there was no discussion of the offending issue, a common occurrence in negotiations. But now Charlene's firm will have to pay the piper in one way or another.*

Cards On The Table

One must be cautious about persons who employ this phrase. Speakers who say "frankly . . . ," or "candidly . . . ," may only be exhibiting bad speech, but the listener must also consider the possibility that previous statements were not true. Use of such words must be considered an attempt at using a tactic. Until convinced otherwise, the wise negotiator should be mindful of the hard bargainer's response which is, "Yes I believe in putting all my cards on the table, provided they are winning ones!"

EXAMPLE *The negotiations are going badly for Yancy who needs to buy certain goods. Nothing seems to nudge Winston in giving concessions needed by yancy. Finally, Yancy tries one more "piece of business." Lowering his voice, he says, "Look Winston, let me be frank, we really want to deal with you because your competitor just doesn't have your reputation on quality. There, I've said it though it puts me at a disadvantage." If that "revelation" impresses Winston, the so-called "cards on the table" are winning ones. But, if Winston is a wise and experienced negotiator, Yancy's statement will be taken with a very large grain of salt by Winston.*

Carrying Words   See Bargaining Chatter

Cherry Picking

Cherry picking occurs when one party negotiates a "package" which the other party accepts, and then selects certain items from the package while rejecting others. This is a questionable ethical practice because it is employed where the selected items in the package have been reduced by the other party but would allow that party to make an overall profit if the rejected items were included. This term is frequently used in political negotiation and has had considerable use in discussions on the Northern Ireland attempted settlements. Cherry picking is also reported in the health field as when an HMO selects the more healthy applicants in its area.

EXAMPLE   *"I'm glad we're getting together. We will: (1) be willing to go for.a price of $896 a unit for sixty-five model 440LR38 compressors, (2) give you a full repair warranty of one year, (3) charge only a $20 deductible for each warranty repair, (4) make delivery in six weeks or less, (5) be permitted to charge you 1% a month interest until paid if our invoice is not paid in 30 days, (6) load your trucks at our dock, (7) receive a 2% price increase on any reorder within three months, and (8) we will supply twenty extra maintenance manuals." "That sounds just great. We have a deal. I am*

so pleased. Ah, just one thing, though. We don't want provisions 3, 5 and 7 included this time. We'll be glad to look at these sorts of terms when we talk about ordering model 660LD40 compressors next month."

Chinese Auction

A party who tries to confuse the opposition, or make them feel insecure, is employing a tactic. For example, telling the other party that he or she has competition is sometimes called the Chinese Auction technique [the origin of the term is obscure]. This conduct is an aggressive act. If this announcement is clothed with a claim that the proposed terms of the other bidder(s) cannot be revealed because of legal reasons (e.g., antitrust, etc.), the pressure is increased. If the target of this tactic decides to play, there are two possibilities. The first is simply to ignore it, treating it either as a bluff or as something one can't do anything about anyhow. The second, if one has or can get useful information, is to estimate the capabilities of the competition and react accordingly.

EXAMPLE   *Palmer has told Harmon that Harmon's price is higher than the competition, but says he can't reveal the actual numbers because "the feds have been getting pretty feisty lately." As it's mid-morning, Harmon suggests a ten-minute break and Palmer agrees. Harmon heads for her office and asks herself, what does she know? First, Palmer is an "old hand" who knows how to play the game. Second, her firm's costs are at least equal to, possibly a bit below, the industry average, and there is no question of quality. Third, there are only two competitors worth worrying about: Belden Products and Jamison Industries. Belden has union problems and is facing a highly probable strike. If there is a problem, it is Jamison Industries. Harmon decides not to play. The break is over and the meeting resumes. Palmer looks up and says, "Well, Ms. Harmon, what say?" Harmon replies, "If we were worried about competition we would have offered you a lower price to begin with to meet it. We're not, and so we didn't. Do you want to discuss delivery schedules?"*

Company Policy

Invoking "company policy" is a practice that shouldn't work. However, it appears to have more success than this simple technique deserves. Its intent is to leverage a weakness into a favorable premise in a negotiation. On the one hand it is not sound strategy to question the other as to why they have such a "stupid" policy, as the ready response of "I am helpless" stymies further discussion. On the other hand it is unwise to take unilateral statements of company policy seriously and to attempt to counter them with arguments or logic. One response which has had some success is, "Well, that may be your policy, but it's not our policy. Now, let's get on with drafting this contract."

EXAMPLE   *Legal doesn't allow that.*

We never agree to pay liquidated damages.

All deliveries are at our dock.

Credit, with discounts, is always a condition on our purchases.

We always charge for maintenance manuals.

Re-orders automatically carry an upcharge.

Our policy allows us 5% returns.

Compromise Solution

The term given to a bargain in which both parties do not get all they wanted in a settlement. Each party had goals which were sacrificed either partly or fully. This is the most common type of negotiation settlement, but it is a "compromise" in name only. It occurs because the original ambition of each party exceeded its grasp. Skillful parties could benefit by mining for other solutions to the task at hand. Such a theory is identified as an "integrative" solution where the parties agree to recognize that there may be a solution offering each more than the current compromise. The challenge is the need to revisit the goals of each negotiator. Here, because certain trust is required, and some candor must be practiced, parties experience difficulty in surrendering control which trust and candor requires.

EXAMPLE   *Toggle needs to purchase an item for $5,000 in order to make a good profit, while seller Melton requires $5,800 for a like result. A compromise solution of, say, $5,400, gives both sides much less than they had hoped to achieve. This is a common sort of outcome for negotiations. Suppose, however, that they decide to try to look for things they might be able to add to the contract. They find that Toggle's trucks coming to Melton's city to pick up purchases have space that could be used to carry 700 pallets Melton has ordered from a supplier in Toggle's city. Shipping the pallets by a for-hire trucker would cost $700. They can share this saving by Melton paying Toggle $350 to carry the pallets. They agree to this; Toggle thus is able to get its item for $5,050 and Melton gets "paid" $5,750.*

Concession Behavior

In the give and take of bargaining sessions, the timing and delivery of the terms and conditions under which one might contract can reveal both intended and unintended strategies. A concession is that part of the give where a party retreats from a previous position to a more favorable stand for the other side. What are the consequences of this move? The pattern of concessions is normally interpreted by the other party as a road map leading to where the parties will ultimately meet. Accordingly, under this view one making concessions must be careful to restrain from giving false signals which will raise the aspiration level of the other side.

EXAMPLE   *Able wishes to buy at $15. Able begins at $11, raises to $12.50, then to $14. This pattern of concession behavior might be reasonably interpreted to indicate that $16 or even $17 is the ultimate goal. A sequence of $11, $12.50, and then $13.50 is considered wiser because the incremental increase becomes narrower (i.e., $1.50, and then $1.00) suggesting that the bidder's price goal resides nearby.*

Conflict Aftermath

This is the academic name given to behavior we all recognize as revenge. Persons who have a strong desire to be liked should consider carefully when choosing the field of contracting and negotiation. At its gut level contracting is not a friendly game. In law, contracting is viewing individuals in the exercise of their acquisitive instinct. Therefore, pleasing the other party at the bargaining table cannot dominate the adept negotiator's thoughts or behavior. On the other hand one cannot practice creating a clear enemy. Strong positions draw resistance and it tests the bargainer's skill to push an advantage only so far. Revenge is a powerful emotion and is ignited where one feels seriously aggrieved. In continuing relationships the exercise of overreaching is restrained by the prospect of future business. However, even in seemingly "one shot" deals an aggrieved party is not

without potential power. Lawsuits, badmouthing, and other unpleasant consequences can easily follow a too one-sided bargain.

EXAMPLE   *In a series of experiments researchers pitted two bargainers against each other in an exercise where the parties needed to cooperate to reach their goals. One side was a stooge who, unknown to the other side, was told to exploit the situation. One set of experiments was staged to give the parties the impression that an audience was watching the bargaining session as voices could be heard behind a one-way glass observation window. The innocent negotiator was made a fool of during a session. This negotiator retaliated even though to do so he "cut off his nose to spite his face." The findings were not surprising. Revenge is appealing when a party is made a fool, and is almost certain if others know about it. Negotiators must be careful when boasting about tough deals struck against unfortunate victims.*

Conflict Management

This phrase has considerable currency in academic circles where researchers attempt to describe the causes of conflict and means for resolving it. Conflict is inherent in business negotiation situations where buying and selling a product or service is involved, but the process itself is designed to resolve the conflict through the creation of a contract.

EXAMPLE   *"But we need a new car, all our friends have one." "Dear, that is very low in the family priorities on our budget." (family conflict) "If we are to upgrade our production this new machine is essential." "Our budget does not allow that capital expense." (intra-company conflict) "We must have delivery not later than four weeks from today." "That's not possible because our production this month is committed to another customer." (purchasing negotiation conflict).*

Cost Analysis

Good preparation includes homework on what the item or service costs in the industry, what firms set the standard for efficient production, and what markups are part of the package. This is necessary whether one is a buyer or seller of goods or services. Not every negotiation can afford even a modest investigative exercise and, at times the cost, even if discovered, may be irrelevant. It is well to consider this last possibility when contracting. Not every seller's offering is determined on cost. Such matters as inventory mistakes (i.e., salvage), buying into the market, or even publicity considerations may be the driving force in the other party's motivation to contract.

EXAMPLE   *Legend has it that this story is true. A widow advertised to sell an expensive car included in her late husband's estate. She sold it for $50. The true value was many thousands of dollars. Neither cost or market value was the relevant point here. Under the provisions of her husband's will the widow had the executrix's duty to sell the car and turn over the proceeds to her husband's previously unknown (to her) mistress. The skillful negotiator will remember the moral.*

Cost Benefit Analysis

This simple exercise is practiced by bargainers in every negotiation, whether consciously or unconsciously. The insightful party looks at costs and benefits in a broad way. What is being given in exchange for what is being offered? Price, financial terms, delivery schedules, and future business are examples of factors to be considered. The skilled negotiator should know the cost and the value of each term in a proposed contract. For example, a particular price may be more than just the price for this deal; it may be a precedent, good or bad, for future deals.

EXAMPLE   *Browder and Mason were experienced negotiators who knew both the value and the cost of the contract terms each customarily offered to the other. Further, because of this, each knew pretty well just about how far he could try to push the other. The result was that they usually had little trouble reaching an agreement both considered to be equitable. However, the situation changed when, with little warning, Browder found himself negotiating with Mason for the purchase of items in a new and very different product line just introduced by Mason's firm. This was a different ball game for both negotiators. Both had to go back to square one, and for some time their negotiations were protracted and difficult as each had to work out new cost benefit analyses related to the new product line.*

Cost Plus Contract

Among the attempts of parties to fairly arrive at a contract figure is the arrangement in which "cost" will be at the risk of the buyer. This is practiced in certain situations for a variety of reasons. It may be that the seller is unable at this time to make a commitment because of a great deal of potential uncertainties involved in the performance. Or, in some industries this is a customary way of doing business. Like all goals, however, there are some serious risks involved here. The method under which "cost" is calculated as well as whether certain items or services should be included must be carefully articulated.

EXAMPLE *A "Hollywood" story should warn contractors about the use of such terms as "cost," "profit" and the like. Particularly when such a word drives the bottom line. A movie star agreed to syndication of his long running TV series. The report noted that the actor struck a generous deal with "72% of the net profits from syndication" to be paid to the actor. Unfortunately the language in the contract identifying the method and items used in calculating "net" profits led to a conclusion in which there were no "net" profits, only "gross" profits that were absorbed by "costs."*

Cultivation

The manner in which a negotiator attempts to establish a favorable environment with another with whom some agreement is sought is, of course, varied. Cultivation includes such simple human expressions as asking about another's family situation, or giving gifts having significant value. State and Federal rules inhibit the latter and the adept bargainer must "know the territory." As an example, Federal courts apply the provisions of the Foreign Corrupt Practices Act (FCPA) to those who attempt to "cultivate" (read bribe) people in other countries who have influence over their government's contracts.

EXAMPLE   *An American aircraft supplier's agent purchased expensive airline tickets for a foreign official and his fiancee. This official could influence the procurement of services by his government. Such conduct is a felony under the provisions of the FCPA. However, a facilitating payment, a customary gratuity given to persuade an official to do more promptly only what he is supposed to do (e.g., process legitimate goods through customs) is acceptable under the FCPA. The legality of seasonal gifts to regular clients and customers depends on their value and specific case law that might be applicable. When a court finds a payment to be what is called a "rebate" or "kickback" the recipient had better be the company and the conduct not be in violation of some local or federal law.*

Deadline Technique

Informing another that something must be done by a date certain is an honorable act in the abstract. All future behavior is subject to time constraints, and its use in negotiation may be sincere. However, it is sometimes used as a tactic to manipulate the other bargainer. When faced with a deadline announcement,

the recipient must decide which intention governs the speaker, and then respond to this demand consistent to one's own objectives and capabilities.

EXAMPLE   *"This proposal is conditioned on acceptance within two days." "Oh, I am sorry. It looks like we can't make a deal!." (Testing the deadline in circumstances where the line in the sand interferes with one's own agenda.)*

Deadlock

Where parties have, with finality, failed to agree on a particular point they are deadlocked. First, in a true deadlock, it may be that preparation by both sides may have been faulty. Simply, one does not wisely expend effort in an adventure that either or both know cannot be achieved. Second, however, one or both of the parties may have attempted to practice a tactic for one of a variety of reasons. These might include a question of publicity, an attempt at softening up the other side for later dealings, or even a ploy to gain company or industry information which can be useful in other negotiations. Apart from these considerations it is generally accepted that a company which dispatches a negotiator to make a deal, but suggests punishment if there is a deadlock, has seriously hampered its agent. Company permission to deadlock, if necessary, is a valuable tool in negotiations.

EXAMPLE   *A bargaining session was proceeding nicely, or so it seemed to Mayu, when the other party started to introduce material demands on items previously not being contested. As the sparring continues Mayu begins to resent the escalation (which see) the other is practicing. Now, items Mayu was previously willing to concede she dispatches as weapons against the other. This "armed conflict" now becomes a matter of unreconcilable positions and only a deadlock will bring relief to both parties.*

Deference

Where a team negotiates it is helpful to know who holds the power. The bargainer may have to exercise some caution lest he or she "plays" to the wrong audience. Perceiving who defers to whom is the duty of all skillful bargainers. However, the bargainer must be aware that some "acting business" may be practiced, similar to the "good cop, bad cop" routine. Mannerisms and other gestures assist in this discovery process.

EXAMPLE   *"Okay, we are all tired so maybe we should have an early break for lunch." It might be fruitful to note who said this, and to have observed what body language was present when the decision to break was made. Further, the behavior of the team members regarding the choice of the restaurant and other aspects of the situation (cars, menu choices, etc.) can be revealing.*

Dickering

Dickering is the process of bargaining involving an exchange of a series of different propositions and bids. In the minds of many it has a negative connotation. Parties make such statements as "I am not a tradesman and refuse to demean myself in engaging in this phony barrage of bids and rejections" or "It is my belief that my words and bid are sincere statements; they are not made to play some sort of game." This criticism has a valid point, but contracting is not a friendly and affable type of conduct. When contracting over uncertain and multiple values, "dickering" naturally occurs.

EXAMPLE   *Marlowe is a gentle, classy individual. In their middle age Marlowe and his wife decide that at last, with the kids gone, they can buy some "decent" furniture by shopping at a fine store. The prices are shocking. Marlowe's wife quietly asks her husband whether maybe they should explain that the price for the sofa is a bit high but they like it. Marlowe explains, that while she was looking at other items he mentioned this and the salesperson was adamant in that the price was fixed. His wife suggests that maybe we should talk to the manager. "No," says Marlowe, "We are not tradesmen, we don't haggle." Marlowe's unconscious snobbery may have been costly.*

Doodling

Parties frequently doodle, that is, make indecipherable scribbles on paper during a business meeting. The general theory is that such behavior indicates boredom. This is of interest only if attention and a favorable response was anticipated by the other party. Doodling is a type of body language and can betray true feelings and attitudes, but also can be just "a piece of show business."

EXAMPLE   *Good lessons about doodling can be learned in committee meetings. There a party can observe any members practicing this conduct. Sometimes the doodler's speech and manner after a period of doodling reveals some insight into his thinking. For examples, doodling may be that party's method of working out some conceptual point, or it may be the doodler's way of formulating what they are going to say when his or her turn comes.*

Doorknob Price   See "Take it or Leave It"

Escalation

This term takes on a ominous meaning when writers comment on negotiation tactics. The authors characterize escalation

behavior as aggressive, if not nasty, in nature. In its basic scenario a session may be developing nicely, if a bit tediously. With a sense of agreement nearly reached one side relaxes. It is at this point when the opposite number practicing this tactic introduces or accentuates an issue seemingly quiescent. This sharp turn can undermine the confidence of the other side and creates an unpleasant atmosphere in the proceedings. Escalation qualifies as a tactic and experienced negotiators quickly identify it as such.

EXAMPLE   *The proposed purchase and sale of a resort hotel was proceeding nicely and the sticking point seemed to be how much credit the buyer would get for replacing the basement boiler. By late Friday afternoon, the parties were tiring and looked to closure. Or so it seemed. The boiler credit was finally agreed upon. A few moments silence. Then the buyer quietly said, "Good, now let's talk about the purchase price." The purchase price had been set "subject to" earlier but had been put aside as matters of multiple credits and debt assumption were resolved, leaving the seller with the reasonable belief that application of these adjustments would simply determine the actual*

*purchase price. The timing of the buyer's statement
under these circumstance qualifies as a really nasty escalation.*

Estimating Wants

Instead of "read my lips," this negotiation advice asks the parties
to "read my mind" as the session gets underway. Negotiation
experts supply interesting anecdotes regarding motivation. Parties sometimes agree or fail to agree for strange reasons. One or
both may probe to find what is holding up agreement or what
brought about unexpected agreement. Because this pursuit may
be a low percentage play, it is better if bargainers simply listen
carefully rather than trying to read minds. Unfortunately, most
of us have little success in discovering true wants, even if such
information would enable our reaching a successful settlement.

EXAMPLE   *Not all negotiators' motivations, or wants, have a financial foundation. Harrison was really "bugging" his opposite number, Gordon, by taking so much time on each
aspect of the negotiation they were conducting in Mobile,
Alabama. By late afternoon it was clear that the meeting
would have to be carried over to the next day. Although
unexpected by him, this caused no hardship for Gordon
who lived in Saraland, a suburb of Mobile. Nor did it
bother Harrison, who lived in San Diego, because he had
already arranged to have a wonderful dinner with his
son and daughter who were a sophomore and senior,
respectively, at Springhill College in Mobile.*

Ethical Contract

There are moral dimensions in addition to legal ones with
respect to behavior while contracting. An ethical contract is one

in which the behavior of the parties, in the light of circumstances, respects human dignity. Here, the study of negotiations finds some conflict when the matter of certain conduct, tactics for example, is used, and is sometimes flat out recommended by writers. Some justify the "play acting" or "pretending" that surrounds much negotiation behavior on the ground that the other side is well aware of what it is and will discount or ignore it. And, there are cultural aspects of bargaining as when a Southern storekeeper would say to Mr. and Mrs. Attila the Hun, "Y'all come back and see us." Some phrases are not expected to be believed. Drawing the ethical line between ethical actions used to persuade others to deal and where overreaching occurs is sometimes difficult.

EXAMPLE   *A contract is ethical where both sides are free and conscious of the implications of their acts: [e.g, each negotiator suffers from no observable mental disorder and appears to free of drugs and alcohol] none have used fraud [e.g, lied about a material point], power [e.g, threat to reveal an embarrassing event], passion [e.g, abetted in assisting the other in his vice] or ignorance [e.g., one party doesn't know a fact which would make the entire transaction worthless to the other] to bring about an agreement which otherwise would have been rejected.*

Excitability

Despite movie scenarios to the contrary, frenetic parties, while uncomfortable to be around, can exercise considerable skill in negotiations. Sometimes the faux pas, a lack of sophistication, and even boorishness can mislead the other party into underestimating the opponent. The basic reason for the success of such parties is that they have selected or fallen into a programmed contracting scenario in which subtlety and poise are not essential.

EXAMPLE   *Harold is a successful negligence attorney and settles 90% of his cases with the adjusters. Cases he does not settle he refers to highly competent trial firms. Harold has a very sharp mind, but has little control over his temper or emotions. He builds his cases carefully. When he negotiates with the adjusters he shows no cool, raises his voice, and speaks rapidly. He seems almost out of control. Adjusters don't like him but Harold does quite well. His negotiation scenario allows for his lack of cool. First, the adjuster must initially deal with him; second, the claims are viable, only amounts are in question; third, he knows how to evaluate a claim and, finally, should no agreement be reached a deadly trial attorney is waiting in the wings. Many car salespersons are beneficiaries of the same programmed contracting scenario. Their lack of poise is not a material detriment in this occupation.*

Experts

In the preparation stage professionals who have competence in a certain area are frequently employed to advise on those aspects of the pending meeting. Sometimes it is necessary for these parties, the experts, to be part of the negotiation team. However, by training they may be somewhat objective and this could cause some difficulties in the haggling session. The team leader must carefully draw the details of the expert's assignment. It may be as straight forward as having the expert look for technical flaws in the other party's presentation of facts, or the expert may take on a more complicated role. If the latter, it may be necessary for the team leader to spell out some of the practical maneuvers of a bargaining session.

EXAMPLE   *Lanning Company has a crackerjack cost accountant. He is somewhat cranky and speaks his mind, whatever the consequences. Lanning's negotiations with a possible contractor require a great deal of expertise in under-standing the accounting methodology to be used in the case of certain expenses of the proposed transaction. Some individuals equate truth with candor. Because the accountant may not have the temperament needed to act effectively in an arm's length setting, his inclusion as a team member may be ill advised.*

Explanation Of Failure

One must be careful not to assume that all pending assign-ments to negotiate will be fulfilled by the signing of a contract. Sometimes, the assignment, or important terms thereof, is doomed from the start, either by reason of impractical expecta-tions or for other causes. The other side, sensing this unreason-able goal by its opponent, is well advised to react to this problem and provide the unsuccessful opponent with a good explanation of the failure of the negotiation. This explanation can be taken back to the opponent's firm, thus saving face for the negotiator and also providing an opportunity for setting a more realistic goal.

EXAMPLE   *Professional contractors know that to be decent human beings is more than a moral imperative; it has business implications as well. The other side in a bargaining ses-sion has an adverse interest but that does not mean that assistance should not be rendered when a deal cannot be made. Simply, one will likely meet these "opponents" again and also they may share their experiences with others. Practical bargainers, sensing failure in the imme-diate transaction, look for an opportunity to give the other side a reason for failure which can be used when opponents report the results to their superiors. It takes lit-tle to offer this sort of explanation: "I am sorry we could not make a deal, but our cost figures at this time have placed us in a position where your offer, reasonable as it is, cannot be accommodated."*

Expected Price

Establishing favorable premises from the beginning is a task worth attempting and a buyer setting an "expected price" is a bit of business that attempts to achieve a negotiation advantage. Assuming that the speaker has done her homework and the price mentioned is reasonable, the practice of aggressively indicating what one expects to pay establishes a premise, which if not quickly and firmly resisted, sets the parameters of the bidding zone that assists the speaker. If the premise—here a price—is unattractive, a quick strike at it must be made. Make no mistake, whether consciously or unconsciously done, this is a tactic in action.

EXAMPLE   *Bransen & Son have always acted as bullies and their behavior has produced a strong position in the industry. They work hard to beat competition and accordingly have been quite successful. Their potential contractors, however, are never too happy with Bransen's initial thrust when buying. "We expect that an order of this size should run $X per unit" is a typical terse statement found both in their verbal communications as well as their written purchase order offers. This type of statement is intimidating under circumstances where the other side believes it is in a position of weakness with respect to Bransen & Son.*

Eye Contact

There are some who can enter a bar or cocktail lounge and have a good idea of which of the opposite sex would be interested in being "chatted up." Here the use of eye contact plays an important role as a first element of an approach to meeting strangers. In negotiation, however, the stage is set for a different type of romance. Here both parties know why they are there, and it is not for fun and games. Eye contact between negotiators is common, even though it tends to create an atmosphere where tactics and other aggressive moves occur and are acceptable. Some believe that failure, or refusal, to make eye contact indicates some negative quality in a person. Yet, not all negotiators make eye contact.

EXAMPLE   *As a youth, Tower worked in a retail shoe store. Naturally shy, his avoidance of eye contact with his customers was easily accommodated as he sat at their feet putting on tryout shoes. He did not change his behavior as he grew older, and evaluating him in a negotiation setting should not lead others to conclude that he is uncertain or untrustworthy; he simply has a life-time habit of not making eye contact. Marylyn makes little eye contact. She found early in life that eye contact intimidated her. She is a good negotiator because she prepares well and has high aspirations. Opposite parties don't understand*

her unwillingness to make eye contact, but accept it, with the wiser ones drawing no conclusions.

Eye Glasses On Table

The meaning of some body language seems more obvious than others. Taking off one's eye glasses, rubbing one's eyes and laying the glasses on the bargaining table seems to say, "I'm tired of the wrangling, things are not going well, and my resistance to the entire project is growing." It is difficult to argue with that interpretation, unless we have an actor among us. Knowledge by the other party that there is resistance should have come earlier than this action, but certainly this is a wake up call to try some new approaches.

EXAMPLE   *Larry has an eyeglass fetish, or so it appears. His habit of taking them off and placing them in view of others is an acquired trait. He uses the glasses in other ways, rubbing his nose with them and the like. It is difficult to read much into these movements that can be useful in negotiations. Many habits have a complicated history. Whether Larry's glasses conduct is feigned, manipulative, or just irrelevant, is a problem only for those whose curiosity wants satisfaction.*

Face Saving

Negotiation is conflict, and managing the resulting friction is the goal of any successful negotiator. Words are spoken during bargaining sessions that either sting or raise the hackles of the other. Many times the words or position taken are not intended as unduly aggressive. Yet, if they cause the recipient of the thrust to look foolish, stupid, or uninformed, he or she will have "lost face," a term not limited to oriental people. Here the prudent bargainer may use some sort of trade off (which see) to repair the damage.

EXAMPLE   *Carlson had a reputation for not suffering fools gladly, and typically spoke his mind bluntly during a negotiation. While negotiating with a three-person team from Dawson Industries he caught one of its members in a really egregious financial calculation error on a major point in the proposed contract. Looking at Slater, who had made the error, Carlson said, "You know, you really don't even belong in this room. You can't even add and subtract simple figures. For your information the correct number is twenty-eight thousand four hundred, not twenty-two thousand three hundred!" Slater cast down his eyes and slumped a bit in his seat. His colleagues looked at him with a combination of annoyance and sympathy. Carlson realized he had gone too far this time and quickly said, "Come to think of it, you all may remember the time last year when I couldn't remember that a gross was 144 items and I started to price my offer as if a gross was 100 and nearly gave the store away." This self-critical comment may repair the damage, or much of it.*

Fair Contract

A contract is "fair" if it appears to be so in the eyes of a beholder. If a person could determine the criteria for "fair" it would be a simple task to measure the facts against the criteria, but there are so such criteria. Each party has its views and reasons which may be solid, flimsy, emotional, or even ridiculous according to the other side. To each party their concerns are real and it would be "fair" to settle on their terms. No one knows what "fair" means, but the word keeps appearing in negotiations. On the other hand, an "ethical contract" (which see) measures bargains from a moral viewpoint.

EXAMPLE *Assume that a seller could produce and market a product profitably for $125, and a prospective buyer would be willing to pay as much as $150 for the product. What would be a fair price, i.e., a fair contract? The answer: any price they agree on. Notice that such a deal could be ethical or unethical depending on whether the criteria measuring morality have been met or not.*

Final Offer

This is a phrase often expressed in bargaining sessions, sometimes dispatched in desperation, irritation or in a drastic attempt to get movement. Parties who tend to exaggerate or lose cool in situations where there is great resistance tend to make a "final offer" impulsively, despite the cautioning of experts and common sense that restraint should prevail unless the speaker is prepared to risk a final rejection.

EXAMPLE *"Jerry, we've acted in good faith, we have met all your criteria, answered all your questions, met all your objections to the extent our firm is able to make a deal, and this is our final offer. . . ." Those not wishing to make a final offer, so to speak, can add a condition or safety valve here. ". . . unless you can come up with an acceptable explanation of your situation . . ." etc.*

Firm Offer

This concept and phrasing may be viewed from several angles. In the colloquial sense it is perceived to be a speaker's wish to be taken seriously with his honor at stake should he renege. Simply, under the legal rules of offer and acceptance, an offer that is "firm" can be taken back, or revoked, prior to some act of approval or acceptance by the other. Under the Uniform Commercial Code, however, professional business persons, i.e., those meeting the requirement of being a "merchant of goods" under the Code, make such statements in writing at their peril. They will be held to that signed offer despite an attempt to change their minds prior to acceptance.

EXAMPLE   *Laura, after several hours of haggling with Allenton, and tired of several seeming reversals of positions during the session, finally demands of Allenton, "Are you really serious about that?" "Of course I am,"responds the other, "You have my word on it, that is a firm offer!" Generally, Allenton's statement is legally risk free until Laura accepts. However, if this statement was made in a signed writing (e.g, quote, etc), the subject matter is a sale of goods, and Allenton deals in such goods (a Code "merchant") Allenton cannot revoke for three months. In international sales, oral statements such as this are irrevocable under the Convention for International Sale of Goods.*

First Offer

Conventional wisdom offers that it is best to refrain from being the first to mention a price in a negotiation. Several reasons are advanced for this counsel. Obviously, the first speaker has committed himself on the upside and that appears settled. Further, there is a matter of apparent power shifting to the silent bargainer. And finally, the price mentioned may come as a pleasant surprise despite some homework and preparation indicating a different opening. Professional buyers consider it to be traditional for the seller to "open the bidding." There are other strategies, however, that do not suggest this practice. The tactic of "bracketing" (which see) for example, requires the more manipulative party to make the first bid.

EXAMPLE   *After some "sparring" over other parts of the proposed transaction and some distractive games (e.g, golf scores,* *industry gossip, etc.) it is time for a price to be mentioned. This can be an important moment. If Glass waits for the other to make a first offer he must be armed with a telling counterattack because Glass suspects the seller's first offer will be near $3,600. Should Glass instead try to diminish the other's expectations by a preemptive strike, such as, "As I understand it, the price could run as high as $3,200, but I will frank with you, that is not in our plan." If Glass does this, he is using the tactic of "bracketing" as a way of making a first offer before the seller makes one.*

Five Percent Rule

In negotiation, as in many other performances, one need only be a little bit better than competition to be considered effective. Some have called that "little" as small as five percent, or even less. In sports, for example, excellence may be easily measured by a stopwatch, ("Folks, Marsa just clipped a tenth of a second off of the world record") or by a judge's tape measuring the length of a javelin throw ("He just set a new world's record!"). A concert violinst either performs to standards monitored by the fine ears of critics or not. The practice of negotiation, however, can't be measured by such accurate and objective, standards. Yet, it would be a very careless management indeed that makes no effort to determine how good a job the firm's negotiator(s) are doing. Some criteria should be established and performance checked against them. These might include briefing on preparation, agreed aspiration levels and associated results, deadlocks and reasons therefore, etc.

EXAMPLE   *Williams is the senior negotiator in his firm's purchasing department. He considers every negotiation, major or minor, to be important and he prepares for each meeting with care. He anticipates and deals easily with the various types of negotiation behavior common in the industry. He keeps himself well informed about factors that may affect price levels of the items his department purchases. It is no wonder that he is a very successful negotiator, and is so regarded by his firm. Yet, all that Williams really has done is ask himself, "What does it take to make a person a good negotiator?" The answer is obvious and it is not rocket science. Achieving a margin of superiority is simply not all that difficult, but many don't take the trouble.*

Flinch

A flinch is an outward manifestation of reaction to the words or behavior of another. A truly "worldly" type is supposed to be able to restrain body language indicating surprise or disapproval when facing outrageous behavior or a surprising event. While many wish to be in control of their outward appearance, bargaining seems full of moments when a party's reaction to a word, gesture or proposition is closely studied by the other party for the purpose of not only reading one's mind, but the lay of the land as well. For this reason it may be useful to "flinch" and appear somewhat "uncool."

EXAMPLE   *Enright is an aggressive negotiator. He believes in expressing his high aspirations by taking an extreme opening position or making an extreme response to the other party's opening position. One party reacted very coolly to Enrights's very high opening offer, simply saying very quietly, "Your offer is preposterous." Enright's reply was, "Sorry, I foolishly assumed that I was in the ball-park!" On another occasion, Enright behaved the same way but got a very different response. The other party leaned forward, nearly out of her seat, and snarled, "If you make one more dumb offer like that, you can stick this deal in your ear! I know the market and you know the market, and you are in Outer Mongolia!" At this, Enright backed off, reduced his offer substantially, and offered an apology for having been far out of line.*

Folded Arms

Unless we are trained actors, some body movements seem to telegraph our feelings or our reactions in situations which include the bargaining milieu. There is a great deal written on the use of hands, arms and the like. Academics and other writers tend to agree that folded arms, the so-called protective stance, is a negative signal to those to whom it is sent.

EXAMPLE   *Barclay was tired. It had been a long day. Most of the terms of the proposed contract had been agreed to. Barclay felt he had been very reasonable in dealing with Jennings, the sales representative of a major machine manufacturer. Only the terms of the warranty remained to be settled. Jennings offered Barclay a limited one-year warranty. Barclay knew absolutely that the industry standard was a two-year comprehensive warranty on that type of machine. He said nothing, just sat back, stared at Jennings, and folded his arms. After nearly two minutes of dead silence, Jennings finally spoke and upgraded his warranty offer to what he knew Barclay expected.*

Forward Movement

A party who moves toward another is either being aggressive or is ready to move forward toward a solution to the issue. The point is that this piece of body language must be viewed in context.

EXAMPLE   *It was late in the day and Joanna believed Ellen, the other party, wanted to finish their discussion and wind up the negotiation. When Joanna made her offer on the final point needing to be considered, Ellen suddenly leaned forward across the table and looked right at her. Joanna was nonplused by Ellen's gesture. What did it mean? How should she respond to it?*

Freebies

A freebie is identified as an extra to a deal garnered without any reciprocal consideration. The so called "trick" to getting something for nothing is based on the premise that the one being asked to add to the other side's goodies will be reluctant to undo a done deal. Some say that the time investment theory (which see) plays a role here. Having spent a lot of time haggling to finally reach closure creates resistance to starting over. Further, the freebie may be a relatively minor item which the other may be willing to surrender. In law, any extras promised after a contract has been made must be supported by consideration unless both parties are merchants (see Uniform Commercial Code).

EXAMPLE   *Some bargainers have a habit of consistently trying to obtain freebies. These could include such things as reducing the purchase quantity required to get a given discount, getting the seller to pay a small portion of the freight charges, the seller being asked to accept returns for up to six weeks instead of a month, and so forth. Some negotiators get well known for this practice and earn nicknames like "Freebie Frank" and "Add on Al."*

Game Playing

Negotiation closely resembles tennis. In tennis a player doesn't always know whether the opponent will "return" a lob, a slice, a cut, or a smash. Not surprisingly, in the heat of a bargaining session a party may forget or be distracted by some emotive "return" by the other, react irrationally, and respond ineffectively. Old sayings about business carry a message of warning, as Carlyle opined that "without some dissimulation no business can be carried on at all," and Maurois stated that "business is a combination of war and sport."

EXAMPLE   *Frederick is a dazzler. He has a running patter, seemingly random, but with a purpose which mixes minor points with major issues. Frederick has been known to spend an inordinate amount of time dealing with the length of a warranty, despite the fact that the cost on the bottom line is not a deal breaker. However, the intensity and interest directed over such minor points disguise his interest in the main points. In a sense he possesses a prepared script for carrying out his mission. If a transaction has a known environment with limited possible moves and situational power for Frederick, he can be quite successful. However, without those constraints in his favor, he must be careful to remember this is a thrust and parry game in which the other party's countermoves are somewhat unpredictable. He cannot afford to be overconfident and underestimate an opponent.*

Generalization

Psychological texts note that the act of generalization is a primary sign of intelligent life, yet the excesses practiced by negotiators in formulating these abstraction lead observers to conclude that too much of a good thing loses its value. Events we experience are singular in nature but that doesn't prevent many from converting these anecdotes into formulae. Generalizations are so common in bargaining chatter that, despite the high probability that most are unfounded, the culture of conversation allows some of these statements to play a role in the contracting process. General statements of policy, practice or intentions should be heard with a cynical and critical ear.

EXAMPLE   *Marian possesses a bundle of "generals" that she lavishly dispenses in her negotiations. She is not embarrassed to be heard saying that "a contractor only disappoints us once," "our system is state of the art," "we never extend credit to first time contractors," and "when parties ask for the names of other contractors we have dealt with we know that they have not done their homework and so we have little interest in doing business with them." She is further been heard to say that "my company never extends credit or agrees to liquidated damage clauses." Despite the banality of these statements some overly sensitive bargainers buy into such messages, so Marian sees no reason to give up using them. In her book, what works, works.*

Goals

Preparation and goal setting are prerequisite to serious bargaining sessions. Yet, the manner in which these are accomplished and objectives are set is not something that can be generalized. An intended goal is the product of the need of the contractors and the abilities, talent and disposition of the agents instructed to perform. In setting goals it sometimes said that the primary negotiation occurs in the agent's company itself, among its managers and the agent. Apart from the specifics of an objective, e.g., A-1 quality pipe, 30 days credit, rejection formulas, etc,, the mind set of the company must be considered. Here, the aspiration level of the corporate culture plays a role.

EXAMPLE   *Levison Fabricating is a very conservative manufacturer, both in finances and operations. This corporate culture permeates Levison's behavior. They negotiate through personnel who are selected for their nature to show restraint and to carry out "reasonable goals" with no attempt to "push the negotiation envelope." It follows that the goals set will likely lie at the moderate range of expectations. The goals set by Levison are easy prey to a bargainer who entertains high aspirations and is able to "read" Levison's approach.*

Good Cop Bad Cop

Despite the obvious "good and bad" behavior of two members of a negotiating team, human nature often rewards those practicing this style. Good cop bad cop conduct is tolerated only where the party being so exposed wants to make a deal with the others. After all, the normal, and sensible, response to the bad cop is to disengage. Those practicing this tactic are attempting to gain one of the main advantages in negotiations, to wit, to diminish the expectations of the other party.

EXAMPLE   *Considerable haggling and much disagreement continued for most of the negotiation session. Benson is beginning to take a fixed position, as he is aggravated by the absence of reasonableness by Frances and her partner. Benson is somewhat irritated by this developing impasse but is quite reluctant to admit a deadlock due to the*

extensive preparation and the time and effort expended so far. Then Frances and Charles, her partner, go into their "act." Charles disgustedly says to Frances, "I told you at the office that this was a waste of time. Benson is not ready for a deal. They just want to scope out the market here. It's clear they feel that they are too big a company for us!" Frances now begins the soothing process, saying "Charles, that is not true, we are just tired, I feel just as confident as I did back at the office that Benson's company would not have expended this valuable time and effort if it wasn't a serious attempt to make a deal !"

Hard Bargaining

Participants in negotiation training sessions are usually reluctant to acknowledge that they practice hard bargaining behavior. While they hold on to secrets, dissemble, execute such tactics as high initial bids, the deadline technique and the like, and never hesitate to use every bit of bargaining power they possess. They still sprinkle such comments as "we are partners," and "we are here for our mutual benefit" in their conversation. It is almost as if bargainers, while denying the presence of "poker" moves, also invoke Seinfeld's coined phrase "Not that there is anything wrong with that." Few bargaining sessions are entirely free of such "schizophrenic" behavior.

EXAMPLE   *Abselson-Lear is a public relations firm whose premier account, Zeta, is expiring. It is now seeking a replacement in Xtal whose agent states the following: "I'll be honest with you. Our management was impressed with the fact that you represent Zeta. We are a conservative firm and they look for safety and how it looks on the outside. To be associated with a firm that has such a client fits into our corporate image." Silence in the face of this statement is hard bargaining. Soft bargaining, if one accepts the premise of some who define that term, would require that Abselson-Lear speak up. These definers would be correct if soft bargaining has as its basis "trust," a frequently cited element in the I win, you win, White Hat, Collaborative or Partner's Theory.*

Hierarchy

Justified or not American negotiators tend to be viewed as "up front, in your face" operators. Accordingly, the identity of the leader in a particular "team" bargaining session is rarely disguised. It may have something to do with the folklore that Americans are not noted for expertise in spying. The frequent traveler needs only to recall the intimate details that airline seat companions, complete strangers, reveal on the short and confined meetings. Nevertheless, the identity of the party calling the

shots is a useful piece of information if only so that one does not err in a presentation. International experts have opinions on the importance of rank among team negotiators. Russia was the obvious example, however even less bureaucratic societies such as England foster the recognition of status and class even in such a particular endeavor as a bargaining session.

EXAMPLE   *Handel considered himself skilled at reading body language. He pays careful attention to reactions of others when he throws "pieces of business" at them. Marylynn was introduced as a junior buyer by Nesbitt, the apparent expert at contracting. Marylynn was reserved, and somewhat deferential on the team. She showed considerable respect for Handel as well as Nesbitt, her "superior." If Handel only observes Nesbitt he may be misreading the situation. Marylynn could be a junior buyer, a witness for other reasons, or even the party with the last word in the session issues.*

High Initial Demands

Despite the risk that an initial aggressive position or demand might offend and so scuttle the favorable impression of reasonableness that one might intend to create, there can be a sound reason justifying the gamble. The tactic of making a high initial bid is dispatched to set up a favorable premise for the user, that of diminished first expectations in the other party. It must be used appropriately, however. First, the marketing environment must be favorable for this maneuver. If industry figures or terms are stable, that is, move within narrow ranges, this tactic will only make the proposer appear ridiculous. Second, a high initial demand must have at least a color of a rationale behind it, such as a change in the market or where a new product or service is touted as being considerably superior. However, making high initial demands is likely to be a poor tactic if used routinely,

especially if it is often followed by a significant reduction as a reaction to the other party's counter offer.

EXAMPLE   *Leonard is a personal injury attorney. He negotiates with claims adjustors. In the very beginning of a case Leonard's task is to make a tentative initial demand when pressed by the adjustor. This demand is always on the high side. Leonard believes this is critical because of a procedure he believes insurance companies set a "reserve figure." If Leonard can influence this amount it becomes much easier to deal with a final settlement. This figure allows companies to informally set aside certain amounts as potential settlements. The particular setting, insurance adjusting, makes Leonard's "high initial demand" appropriate.*

High Probability

A skilled negotiator will carefully assess the probability that a particular negotiating tactic or strategy will be successful. The assessment will take into consideration relevant factors that apply in a given situation. These could include past negotiation experience with the other firm and its negotiators, current general business conditions, current industry conditions, any secret or inside knowledge about the other firm, the situation of the negotiator's own firm, the venue of the meeting, and so forth. But, even if a conscientious and careful assessment has been made, few things in life are certain, and choosing the approach to be used in a particular negotiation is, simply, a judgment call.

EXAMPLE   *During the past two years Helen had negotiated half a dozen contracts with the Lanning Company's sales department and had gotten most of what she wanted each time. She had another meeting with the Lanning people scheduled for the next week. However, this time an amount in the neighborhood of $700,000 would be involved, nearly six times as much money as in any of her previous negotiations with Lanning. The other contracts had been for manufacturing consumables; this one would involve purchase of heavy-duty forklifts. And, when she received a phone call from Lanning's sales office about the upcoming meeting, the sales secretary mentioned that Lanning would be represented by Ms. Madeline McMillan, a person whom she had never met. Further, the meeting was scheduled to be held in Lanning's Engineering Department, rather than in its sales offices where Helen's previous buying meetings had been held. Helen was an intelligent person, and she realized that this time it would not be wise to depend on her previous experience in negotiating with Lanning. She would have to tailor a different approach.*

Hills To Die On

Where there is human discourse, conflict sometimes arises and parties may get sidetracked or wander down irritating and non-productive alleys. A cranky dispute over such things as a warranty term or a proposed charge may trigger a temptation to take a fixed position and fight. It is at these times the big picture must be seen and the offended party must determine whether this is the place to take a stand. So to with blatant falsehoods that appear from time to time out of the mouths of negotiators. Only if such statements are relevant to the progress of the negotiations should they be challenged. One is trying to persuade, not win an argument.

EXAMPLE   *Harbill, who represented Bollard Industries, was negotiating a contract for the sale of six mixing machines to Carlson who represented the buyer, Lockridge Company. Price had been agreed and most minor differences had been worked out. But, a stumbling block had developed over the warranty. In previous sales for very similar machines Bollard had given a three-year warranty, but for this new model the warranty offered was 27 months. Carlson was adamant that a three-year warranty be put in the contract, but Harbill would not budge. Carlson had really expected a three-year warranty and asked Harbill why the change in policy. Harbill replied that this model would very likely get hard use and this justified a shorter warranty period. And, he could not even trade a small price increase for a longer warranty, explaining that marketing would get the credit for the sales price, but engineering would incur the costs of warranty repairs and engineering had made their position very clear on that point. Carlson knew he could buy almost exactly the same machine from a Bollard Industries' competitor and for the same price, and likely with a three-year warranty, although the latter was not certain. But, going to a competitor carried risks as it would mean doing business with a new vendor and, of course, there would surely be a delivery-date delay. Carlson considered the situation. Bollard could meet the specified delivery*

*date and the price was right. The only problem was the
length of the warranty. Going to a competitor was feasible, but that had some disadvantages. A 27-month warranty v. a 36-month warranty. Was this a hill to die on?*

Impossible Offers

Despite the obviousness of the practice, parties will make presentations which they should know are ridiculous and totally
unacceptable to the other side. Anecdotes are frequently cited to
confirm such behavior. Strangely enough, an impossible position may continue to be pressed despite the fact that this may
make negotiations persist for several meetings. Why might such
extremes be ignored by the other side? The short answer may be
that although both parties are aware of the needs (or situation)
of the other, they refrain from commenting on this reality, relying instead on the fact that both parties have not left the table
despite a stalemate.

EXAMPLE   *An ocean shipping carrier ordered two tankers from a foreign shipbuilder, placing a considerable down payment
pending construction and delivery. The tanker market*

"tanked." The carrier now needs to cancel and retrieve part or all of the down payment. The builder insists on full performance of the contract. This type of negotiation is called a "work out" in the banking community and known as a "conversion" in the shipping business. Such a bargaining situation is likely to be extended over several days, weeks, or even months, with each side pressing "seriously" its position, i.e., that the builder will take no less than full payment while the carrier demands the complete return of the down payment. Although this behavior tests each (the wear-down principle), the situation is such that each must ultimately, in the light of economic reality and the position of both parties, drop its impossible demands and start negotiating to reach a solution. The alternative is to submit the dispute to the tender mercies of the courts with all the outcome uncertainty and costs attendant with legal action, or to submit the matter to an arbitrator if the contract so provides.

Industry Pricing

Inexperienced negotiators need to be on constant guard for those silent premises which will undermine one's bargaining power. Proffered industry pricing (or other data) is one such premise. Where the figures, terms or practices supposedly extant in the "industry" are favorable to the other side one can be assured that they will be advanced in the sessions. However, verification of these pieces of information is frequently unavailable at the time and place of the session. It is safest to be indifferent to these attempts by the other side to lower your expectations when they pronounce what the market or industry "realities" are.

EXAMPLE   *"But don't you see, Marlene, that your figures are totally out of market. The latest Smedley Report I've seen clearly shows not only that the industry amounts are far from your position as well as graphically showing the present trends in our market area are on a downswing!"*

"What I see, Charlie, is a total lack of response by you to my very reasonable offer for six hundred units at seventy dollars a unit, delivery in three weeks, freight prepaid, and no charge for returns of up to ten percent. Stuff that in your Smedley Report!"

Inside Information

Good preparation, or perhaps the product of some previous negotiation, and sometimes accident, may bring inside information about the other side's needs, weaknesses, or business situation. Such information can be beneficial, but even skilled negotiators may be tricked by its presence (See Secret Information). The subtle point about inside information is that it can sometimes turn on the possessor.

EXAMPLE   *In mock negotiation exercises the "mattress spring" hypothetical has been used for years at in-plant training programs to drill first time negotiators on this point. The buyer, who manufactures both springs and mattresses, needs a special oversize mattress spring for its fall mattress campaign. Its spring manufacturing division is about to go on strike so the buyer looks for another maker to assure availability. The buyer therefore "knows" the manufacturing cost for these oversize springs. Accordingly, the buyer in effect has "inside information" which, as the exercises play out does them harm because all but the careful are already prepared to negotiate near the "cost" basis. The exercise, i.e., the hypothetical facts, is set up so that the seller has made a production mistake, which, unknown to the buyer, has placed the seller in a position where they may have to sell the oversize mattress springs for salvage, a sum considerably less than the cost* basis. *In twenty years of administering this exercise less than 10% of the mock buyers settled with a price between the salvage (junk) value and the cost basis. Thus, buyers' inside information can be harmful, rather than beneficial, for inexperienced participants.*

Integrative Solution

It seems fair to assume that if two reasonable parties meet to solve a problem they are likely to find a way. However, even if all negotiators were born "reasonable" in makeup there are times and situations where this common search for agreement is hindered. The trick for those who advocate seeking an integrative solution is to recognize the need for the cooperative effort of both bargainers to setting aside existing positions or goals that each had entertained. Instead, they need to seek a solution that accommodates the needs of both parties. Arguably, this may not always be possible, but the value of an integrative solution makes it worthwhile trying hard to find one.

EXAMPLE   *Mallory Trucking Company was a truckload carrier handling about 50 truckload shipments a year for Raton Manufacturing, Inc. from Raton's plant in Denver to Chicago. This was a nearly 100% increase from the previous year. Raton argued that this number of shipments warranted a reduction in Mallory's freight charges. Mallory said a reduction might be possible if Raton were to schedule its shipments to leave the same day and time each week; this would enable Mallory to schedule its equipment more efficiently. Raton said it would cost it at least $100 per shipment in shipping department overtime pay to do this. Mallory considered this along with its saving of $200 a shipment if Raton followed a weekly "set" schedule. Mallory then offered Raton an integrative solution: follow the "set" schedule and we will give you*

$150 of our savings to offset your $100 overtime cost and we will each come out $50 per shipment ahead, which will be $2,500 more in annual profit for each of us.

Last Offer Best Offer

In modern litigation some courts have established a mediation system requiring certain types of cases to be assigned to a mediator prior to setting the dispute in actual trial. The mediator, usually a lawyer trained in this area and appointed by the judge, attempts to unravel the competing claims. Each party may be invited to submit its "last and best offer" in writing to the mediator. This tests the skill of the negotiators who must attempt to shape their last and best offer taking into consideration the possible offer of the opposition and the attractiveness of each offer to a third party. The mediator reviews each side's offer, talks to both sides privately and tries to explain the realities including the costs of courtroom litigation as well as the uncertainties of a trial's outcome. The parties may then come to an agreement. If not, the mediator reports failure to the court and a trial will be set.

EXAMPLE   *Simpson Company and Torman Products have contracted with each other but are now bogged down on a breach of contract issue, each accusing the other of misrepresentation, obfuscation, and even downright lying. Things have gone from bad to worse. Torman operates its production lines on a just-in-time basis, and the dispute centers on a provision in the contract providing for significant liquidated damages in the event of late delivery. Another provision of the contract provides that failure of any aspect of performance is excused if it is due to an Act of God or for any other reason beyond the control of the seller. The event triggering the dispute was a snowstorm which Simpson says clearly justified the delayed arrival of Simpson's shipment to Torman's plant. Simpson has invoked the Act of God provision of the contract, pointing out that the snowstorm was an Act of God and certainly beyond its control. However, Torman's purchasing manager has consulted with the dispatcher at a trucking company that operates schedules over the same highway route used by Simpson for its shipments to Torman. The dispatcher at this company says their trucks encountered no delays due to the snowstorm. Simpson's dispatcher has replied that this competitor has a lousy safety record, often operates under dangerous weather conditions, and just wants to get some of Torman's business. At loggerheads, Simpson and Torman each submitted their last and best offer to a court-appointed mediator. Simpson wants the Act of God clause applied, and Torman relies on the experience of Simpson's competitor as showing Simpson could have performed. The mediator is unable to bring the parties together, and the case will go to trial.*

Lawyer Negotiators

A legal education rarely implants meekness in students. Yet, because attorneys employ the language of persuasion (aimed at juries and judges) it is easy to understand why they might presume to profess skill in negotiation. Yet the environment in negotiations does not match what an advocate does in the practice of law. In litigation, for example, the format allows certain behavior which would be anathema to a business settlement. Each attorney is permitted to press his position to the extreme, no matter how insulting it may be to the other side. Further, lawsuits are generally zero sum games; either the plaintiff or defendant wins, completely in most cases. A precontractual discussion can hardly tolerate such patent aggression, no matter how strongly each bargainer may internally feel in a particular bargaining session. Accordingly, the use of a lawyer in negotiations carries a few practical caveats. First, of course, is the selection of an attorney who appreciates the different environment and can accommodate their technique to it. Settling a case for a client, for example, is a "one shot" negotiation, where restraint is rarely practiced but is necessary in a business relationship where one will meet the opposite number again. Further, certain types of contracting do not lend themselves to heavy "lawyering."

EXAMPLE   *Accurara Corporation had three major matters to negotiate. The first is an extension agreement with its major
bank lender, second the purchase of heavy equipment,
and third a cooperative relationship with a research
partner. Because some of the major loan provisions are
highly technical, considerable lawyering might be
required here. This would be less so in the purchase of
heavy equipment except at the final stages. However, the
sessions with a prospective research partner will be very
sensitive to a heavy negotiation hand, a trademark of
some lawyers. In those types of arrangements where both
parties are not yet sure where they are going, and given
the lack of specificity as to objectives and undertakings,
the negotiators must practice a more open and trusting
behavior. Unless the lawyers have been trained in taking
a constructive part in such a negotiating environment,
there is a tendency for them to attempt to drive too hard
and too specific a bargain.*

Lecturers

Few abandon long-practiced presentation styles unless they have heard themselves objectively or have been professionally evaluated. While words and their phrasing can persuade others, artful or clever language skills without an attractive cadence or "attitude" that assists in improving one's bargaining position are misused jewels. The old saw has meaning here: it is not always what one says, but how it is said. Those that lecture outside of a classroom run the risk of offending others without redeeming tradeoffs. However, some situations are more forgiving of this style, particularly if the "lecturer" is able to appeal to another party's need or problem. Many can recall Professor Harold Hill's lecture about all the evils faced by the residents of River City and how a boys' band would solve them in the Broadway musical The Music Man: "You've got trouble right here in River City . . ." went the lecture. The result, among other things, was the sale of a lot of band instruments to the local residents.

EXAMPLE   *Barry plays the role of the stereotypical "encyclopedia salesperson." He comes on strong with a well prepared lecture once his foot is in the door. His audience is pre-selected, a family with school-age children and thus*

*attentive to children's learning needs. He is quite suc-
cessful in persuading families to sign up for this educa-
tional opportunity after being lectured to as to the
value of knowledge, particularly for their young.*

Legal Words

Effective bargainers understand language and are careful to use
words properly. Properly includes avoidance of terms which
have a special meaning in business. It is all very well to "offer"
one's sympathy, one's assistance, and so on. It is another to use
the word "offer," for example, while dealing with a prospective
contractor. So are the other technical words of contracting, such
as accept, counteroffer, and reject. A common habit of some
business people is their free use of the word "partner." This
word should be avoided unless one really intends the legal con-
sequence this word signifies. Some parties incorporate but still
continue to call their fellow shareholders as partners. In a legal
dispute such a designation could be expensive. So too with other
legal words.

EXAMPLE   *Hansin was disgusted with the course of her contract
with Laslow. It has turned out to be a unprofitable relationship and Hansin, in a fit of frustration, wrote Laslow
that she "canceled" the contract. Unless there was some
provision in the agreement that defined and permitted
cancellation, the use of this word may be deadly notice
that she "is breaching the contract."*

Legitimacy

Those who contend that certain business documents carry psychological weight use the term "legitimacy" in their explanation.
Thus, catalogs, price lists, standard forms, posted notices and
various other types of documents are intended to impress or

intimidate others, permitting the owners to point to "official" policy. It follows that company proposals on printed company forms do intimidate some people. Experienced negotiators are not so intimidated yet, employ the devices themselves.

EXAMPLE   *Beverly Fabricators are great believers in the printed word. Its work offices contain many signs setting forth the do's and don't of company behavior. Their form contract for their suppliers has in its heading the words:* **THESE ARE OUR TERMS - THEY ARE FAIR AND THEY ARE NON NEGOTIABLE.** *The firm is enthusiastic over the power of legitimacy and worships at its shrine. Unfortunately, its prayers will not be answered by experienced negotiators from other firms.*

Letter Of Intent

A common problem for some companies is how to reach "agreement" over a matter not clearly capable of exact determination, or where either or both parties don't wish to be legally bound.

Or, a party may wish to have some sort of commitment from another while not wishing to be bound themselves. The legal system does not permit this and some parties are also reluctant to make promises if only they have ethical but not legal obligations. In a simple example a party may wish that another be prepared to perform as soon as a binding contract can be entered into. Thus, the negotiator may attempt to induce the other to purchase supplies, hire personnel or whatever, in anticipation of a future order, i.e., contract, thus not wasting lead time. So a "letter of intent" might be signed. In this instance a writer might indicate that "while the budget is not yet available for this order it is the writer's sincere belief that when the expenditure is authorized we must proceed quickly toward performance." This is a letter of intent, having little weight except in the ethical environment. More complicated letters are drafted by experts when companies are engaged in projects where at the moment neither party can know exactly the details or "bottom line" regarding commitments. In order to assure that a "letter of intent" (or whatever the parties title their document) does not prove a contract, words like "The parties do not intend to contract at this time and the statements and signatures herein contained do not constitute a legally binding agreement." Courts have had to struggle with documents that do not contain such a statement, examining the wording to determine whether a binding agreement exists. Obviously, negotiators are reluctant to include such a clear disclaimer of legality after struggling to reach some sort of "understanding."

EXAMPLE   *A manufacturer of a "revolutionary" style of cooking pan negotiated with a marketer who used TV to sell products. The marketer requires all products to be unique so that they "cannot be purchased in stores," a practice that aids in selling. A well drafted two-page "Letter of Intent" was prepared by the attorneys for the firms. In some places exclusivity was agreed to, in other parts there was some contrary language. Further, the quantity of pans to be manufactured over time was*

*expressed in indefinite language. When the manufac-
turer later balked over a demand by the other a law
suit ensued. The appeal court took six pages of discourse to evaluate the language and came to the conclusion that the agreements of the parties over several
critical aspects of the deal were too indefinite for a
court to enforce. The court ruled that the letter did not
evidence a contract. Had the parties a clause indicating no contractual intent such review would have been
unnecessary. However, the parties did intend a serious
undertaking and wanted to do business, yet the uncertainties of each in several aspects led them to include
language of indecision.*

Level Of Aspiration

Successful negotiators understand that having high aspirations
is a concept of great importance in achieving good negotiation
results. The literature suggests that without such ambition a
bargainer lacks the necessary spark to achieve a successful negotiation result. High aspirations must, of course, be based on a
reasonable appreciation of business reality.

EXAMPLE   *Talbert had read in an article in a business magazine
that the market prices for an item he was to purchase
ranged from $40,000 to $43,000. Talbert did not check
this information to determine whether (a) it was true,
and b) whether it was relevant to his firm's need for quick
delivery. If Talbert wishes to practice as a river boat gambler and just "try out $34,000 as a first bid," he may find
himself out in left field looking pretty stupid. Setting an
aspiration level out of thin air is risky. Having a high
level of aspiration is good practice, but it has to be based
on carefully gathered and evaluated information, not on
hope, extreme confidence in own's own ability, or having
faith in one's luck.*

Limited Menu

In many negotiations there are some potential items that a bargainer wishes to avoid. Either they are perceived weaknesses or terms (or matters) that one party does not intend to offer the other. Limited menu is so named because of the deliberate effort of the negotiator to take pains to develop a scheme which avoids these confrontations. In its basic sense the technique also cleverly aims at avoiding the principal weakness in a meeting.

EXAMPLE   *Having helped the customer to try on several suits at the men's clothing store, the salesperson now asks the customer, "Sir, do you want both the blue and the brown suit or just the blue one?" This old sales technique illustrates the basic ingredient which is the multiple choice question, cleverly omitting the "none of these." option.*

Linkage

In antitrust law the term linkage refers to a tying arrangement. In negotiations the term is broader and includes the attempted application of the psychological tactic of coupling certain understandings and items in order to bring about a desired result. The object under consideration can be as ephemeral as an assurance of a "long term relationship" to a demand in more concrete terms announcing that the deal is contingent on the acquiescence to another term or matter which commonly the other party is less than eager to agree to.

EXAMPLE   *Barrow, a wholesaler of garage doors, has a business arrangement with the manufacturer of electronic garage door openers. Barrow is a popular and successful supplier in the area and insists that its retail dealers also buy the openers when buying garage doors. This is a tying arrangement, which, depending on market dominance might be an illegal practice under antitrust law. When*

bargainers attempt to couple the subject matter of a deal with other considerations they are attempting "linkage," a popular practice both in business and politics.

List Price

Many companies' catalogs or other documents contain what are labeled as list prices for the firm's products. These prices are seldom the actual prices at which the firms' goods are sold. Rather, they function as a point of departure for discounts based on quantity, financing, or other [negotiated] terms. Some companies make a practice of gathering "list price data" for use by their negotiators, but extreme variances among companies with respect to discount schedules, for example, make such information of little value.

EXAMPLE *Aannit Industries experienced some uncomfortable antitrust experience because of the aggressive behavior of its purchasing agents. The new purchasing manual now requires that agents in acquiring raw material from vendors may not consider a bid which is less or more than 10% of the "average list price of the goods." In order to find such averages clerks at Aannit telephone different vendors across the country for their present list prices. These inquiries are "duly recorded" despite any attempt to determine their accuracy as a selling price for the material.*

Long Term Relationships

This phrase has several meanings. First, it simply describes conduct in which two firms have made a practice of dealing with each other over a significant time period. The phrase also has currency as a tactic in bargaining sessions as one party asks for concessions because "we are looking forward to a long term relationship." This prospect of future business is received skeptically by experienced negotiators.

EXAMPLE   *In mock negotiation exercises the "mattress spring" hypothetical has been used for years at in plant training programs to drill first time negotiators on certain negotiation tactics. The buyer, who manufactures both springs and mattresses, needs a special overside mattress spring for its upcoming mattress sales campaign. It's spring manufacturing division is about to go on strike so the buyer looks for another maker to assure delivery. This is to the buyer, of course, a one time purchase. Yet the participants in this exercise occasionally and sometimes shamelessly press the point that a good price is necessary "this one time" as future orders could be forthcoming. The ethicist examines the type of language used by these buyers. Accordingly, for the careful speaker the truth need not be sacrificed if there is a future prospect that has reality. For example, in answering the seller's question as to why future business would be forthcoming since the buyer makes its own springs, some buyers (participants) respond by saying, "yes, we also manufacture such springs but is always prudent to have a second source which is why we are here today." Such an answer can be based on the true possibility and so allows the ethical speaker to still be an effective negotiator.*

Lowballing

This term is used to describe several different types of conduct. However, in negotiations the common thread is the appearance of an unexpected favorable term from one's opponent. Several motivations fuel this tactic. One, the other party needs a contract badly. This need may be to keep the plant busy, the other's bank demands to see orders, or they are in financial trouble and any business is good business at this stage. Two, a softening-up procedure is being attempted. The other party is relying on the time investment theory (which see) to assist this move. The appearance of the favorable term or offer is only that, a brief appearance. As things progress in the session, it appears that these favorable items cannot be signed off on. Third, the party wishes to buy into your business and is willing to take a loss in the beginning or, more frequently, has ways of gaining extras on the deal because they know more about their product or service than you do. And lastly, and perhaps the most deadly of all, is the intention of the other side to indeed contract on these terms,

and then later breach the contract. This is not an uncommon experience in modern practice.

EXAMPLE   *The Buyer has several firms to choose from but the Seller has just made a great offer. It substantially beats the others. Surprisingly, the Seller does indeed contract. Lead time is an important element in the contract. One month before time of delivery the Seller notifies the Buyer, apologizing, stating, "Sorry, Mate, we just can't deliver at that price." "But you agreed; we could sue your pants off!." "Yes," the Seller replies, "You have every right to do so but that is the way it is. Now, if you could just add 10% to the price we can get right on it." The Buyer may have to bite the bullet this time, but the Seller will have to deal with any repercussions of its action in the marketplace.*

Low Probability

Estimates of probable success or failure are called probabilities in negotiation. Clearly, a negotiator wants to succeed rather than fail, so the objective is to avoid adopting a strategy that has a greater chance of failure than success.

EXAMPLE   *Damon had enjoyed considerable success in negotiating contracts for the purchase of parts from a variety of small vendors to whom his firm's business was important. Damon's firm had recently developed a new type of pump for which it was receiving very large orders from its distributors. This pump required a purchased part (a bearing), and the quantities of this part that would be needed could not be supplied by the small vendors with whom Damon had been dealing. There were three potential vendors for this bearing: all were very large companies. Damon was assigned the task of negotiating for the purchase of these bearings and he viewed the assignment as routine. He was shocked when his negotiations with the first two of these vendors ended in deadlock; neither would deliver at anything close to his expected price. As he contemplated his upcoming meeting with the third firm, he knew that his strategy of negotiation which had worked so well with small firms had not worked at all with two very large ones.*

Lying

A negotiator has several options in regard to tendered falsehoods. She may appear to ignore them, or challenge the speaker, or even respond with an obvious lie of her own. The first choice is preferable when the assertion does not rise to the level of importance upon which a decision must be based. The second is confrontational, but may be a desirable choice if the lie can be refuted easily. The third choice is a means for saying, in effect, let's stop the nonsense and get back to business. Negotiators in training sessions tend to express outrage during the "critique" program by claiming that the other side "lied" about a point during the bargaining give and take.

EXAMPLE   *In mock negotiation exercises the "mattress spring" hypothetical has been used for years at in plant training programs to drill first time negotiators on certain negotiation situations and tactics. The buyer, who manufactures both springs and mattresses, needs a special oversize mattress spring for its upcoming mattress sales campaign. It's spring manufacturing division is about to go on strike so the buyer looks for another maker to assure delivery. Of course this circumstance is potentially a weakness in the buyer's position. Obviously if the sellers have done their homework they would know that the buyers make the very product that they are attempting to purchase. What does the truthful speaker say when the obvious question is asked: "Why come to us for the bed springs when you make them yourselves?" The participants in the mock exercise must appreciate the difference between candor and the truth. Just because a question is asked does not mean that it must be answered. Some participants recognize this difference and where they do speak they meet it cautiously, protecting the privacy of their business affairs. Some say that there "has been a blip in production" and leave it at that. That is not a lie, a strike is indeed "a blip in production."*

Machiavellianism

Because of the writings of Nicolo Machiavelli [1469-1527] in which he described the political machinations of renaissance Italian princes, negotiation researchers often use his name to describe a party who has great confidence in his or her ability to persuade others. Academics call this trait an individual's generalized belief of social influence. Self confidence in one's ability, so goes the lesson, provided it is founded on past successes, gives the edge to such individuals in bargaining even where an objective analysis of a pending session suggests difficulties for these parties.

EXAMPLE   *Margaret has told her mother from early years that she is insecure, that she believes everyone is smarter than her, more assured than her and better liked. But Margaret had a strong will despite this poor self-opinion. She learned to pretend the opposite, but only with fragments of her life. Contracting with others was one such exception. As a child she picked up two points from her mother's one year in college which included Psychology 101. First, the movers in this world have a vision of success. Second, the doctrine of pretend. She wanted to see how well she could act confident, self-assured, even cocky. At first it was a trick, but despite her low self-esteem she was able to put the effect of her usual self-evaluation on hold when doing her job as a manufacturer's agent. The pretend maxim learned at her mother's knee seemed to work for her and she seized it: "Go through the motions and the proper emotion will follow." She still whines to herself that she has low esteem, but her "business act" is so developed that while on stage at the bargaining table, she exudes sufficient confidence to persuade others.*

Major Points

All but simple negotiations have multiple issues to settle. Some issues, or points, are more important than others but are not always recognized in the beginning. Typically, major points are usually decreed by the negotiator's superior. At the bargaining table, however, the decision of the competing parties to reveal and sequence the appearance of these major points is a complicated one. Like a courtroom dilemma as to which witnesses to put on first, the decision-maker must simply "see how it goes."

EXAMPLE   *Some tacticians believe that the major points should be addressed in the beginning. Larson always quickly put all his face cards on the table. Larson has an aggressive manner, and while very clever is low on patience. Because he represents a firm which has substantial leverage due to the firm's dominating position in the market, his rashness does little damage to the possible outcome. He could continue to believe that bringing the major points to issue early is a winning technique. However, dealing with big issues first hinders full development of the investigatory stage in a negotiation. Small issues or points can be introduced and pressed to measure both the competence and interest of the opposition as well as lead to the possible discovery of new relevant information. Larson is getting good deals. He might be able to get better ones.*

Make Or Buy

To the bargainer the relevance of the make or buy concept is in its possible use when faced with an opponent who appears to have little competition. In this application, it qualifies as a tactic.

EXAMPLE   *Packit Company has found fewer and fewer suppliers of a particular assortment of field valves it needs. The news just got worse. Its long term supplier has just purchased*

its major competitor, a firm that Packit was able to use in negotiations when their usual supplier became too greedy. Packit now must say that it is actively considering making these field valves, thus alerting the supplier that there is a possibility of a new "competitor," namely Packit itself. However, the "threat" must be realistic if it is to be effective. If, for example, making the field valves would require Packit to invest in and build a major manufacturing facility, any threat to make these field valves would be hollow. Conversely, if Packit could, in fact, relatively easily produce its own field valves, the threat would have real substance.

Maneuver

There is no common understanding for this term. Some call it a move that qualifies as a tactic. To others the word seems less aggressive. See the discussion on Tactics.

Market

At old English law the term *market* referred to a price or term arrived at by willing buyers and sellers. At law today the precise figure or term is determined by a trier of fact who, hearing evidence of what these two hypothetical persons would set, then determines from this evidence a price or term. The evidence would include past sales of like goods, when and where sold, advertised prices, governmental indexes and other statistical data.

EXAMPLE   *"You just haven't been out there if you think that my price is high. The market is that tight and this figure is in line with others." "You may be right but I need a few more specifics on this. Could you show me your recent invoices?" "I know I sound skeptical but Cameron, my*

*five year old son (with an ingratiating smile), taught me
something the other day. I wanted him to eat his spinach
and he resisted. I then stated that millions of little Chinese boys would love to have that spinach. Cameron then
asked me 'to name two.'"*

Matter Of Fact

Like the poor mentioned in the bible, speakers who use this
phrase will always be with us. It is an attractive phrase especially
since in many contexts something is indeed a matter of fact. On
the other hand it may simply be an attempt to create strength
out of thin air. One is reminded of the dairyman Tevye in the
musical Fiddler on the Roof who was fond of invoking biblical
authority with the prefix statement, "As the Good Book says . . ."
when often it said no such thing. When it comes to negotiation
it is difficult to establish a "fact" if there is any room at all for
differences of opinion or interpretation.

EXAMPLE *Nick was a small town politician until he was "retired"
from office. He really had a spiel. Some called him "Sen-
ator Foghorn," but not to his face. His connections
earned him a job as a negotiator. His old patter never left
him. "As a matter of fact," he would opine, "our service is
the finest in the market." The bargainer has several
responses to this. Ignore the nonsense if there is no merit
in pursuing the issue, or carefully use it as means of finding out things, beside the obvious fact that Nick lacks
class. "That is a matter of fact, is it? Great, that's just
what my company needs to know. What criteria are
being used to determine this? Our marketing people
could incorporate that data in their presentation." Such
a response has risks, but when it is necessary to reduce
the expectations of the other side such an approach may
even things up a bit.*

Maximize Profits

This seemingly innocent phrase can be of considerable relevance to the negotiator. While the casual use of it in directing one's agents to so perform is harmless, it is not helpful unless some specificity is added to the phrase. When goals are not specific or sufficiently high bargainers tend to make concessions too quickly or make inadequate compromises.

EXAMPLE   *Velume Inc. finally recognized that vague instructions to its agents were permitting a casual "shoot from the hip" attitude during their negotiations. Reviewing the situation, they discovered that when a specific profit goal was prescribed their negotiators were more likely to devise and employ innovative moves to attain that objective.*

Minimize Losses

The instruction to a negotiator to minimize losses is sometimes given, but many view it as a losing proposition in most cases because it creates a negative frame of mind which is scarcely desirable in a negotiator. However, there are situations in which it may be viewed as an appropriate instruction.

EXAMPLE   *Walker Corporation had developed a new product line and, as a result, had a large inventory of obsolete parts. Walker's VP Finance knew these parts were now simply scrap. His instruction to the company's negotiator was "Check with every scrap dealer within the metro area, and find the one whose price will minimize our loss on this stuff."*

Minor Breach

Instead of whining over one's disappointment with minor breaches committed by a contractor, an executive should look

upon such unfortunate happenings as possibly offering oppor-
tunities. Minor breaches of a contract do not, contrary to popular belief, authorize the innocent firm to call off the whole deal.
Even if it did, only a lawsuit could settle the issue, a course of
action that few business firms find it useful to pursue. Minor
breaches occur during the post contracting phrase, are not
uncommon events, and can often be used effectively as trade off
items (which see).

EXAMPLE   *Lanning & Son engaged a public relations firm (PR)*
under a two-year contract to provide certain publicity
services including provisions requiring (1) publication of
two specific publicity pieces in certain trade journals,
(2) an association newsletter, and (3) a publicity piece
mentioning the president's role in local charities. PR
delivered on the first two specifications but not the char-
ity item. This last promise was a "bone" offered by PR
and was not something that Lanning had sought, but
they were pleased with the item. Should there be any
problems with the contract caused by Lanning & Son,
this "minor breach of contract" could be a factor in the
bargaining process.

Missing Element

A negotiator who during sessions, or arranging for bargaining
sessions, somehow disappoints in providing a necessary person,
document, commitment, or whatever to advance or consum-
mate the deal is employing one of the most common tactics.
This conduct is sometimes called the missing man maneuver.
Such practitioners are "pulling the other's chain." The intent of
this tactic could be an attempt to soften up the opposition, or to
execute the "time investment" tactic (which see), or as a valuable
"delaying" chip if negotiating with another regarding the same
subject matter. It is a tactic that can only be used once with

another party (unless that party is exceptionally naive), and it may also create an undesirable industry reputation if the offended party spreads the word about what happened.

EXAMPLE   *A Miami attorney owned undeveloped commercial land. He was generally a cool negotiator but the carrot offered by the Chicago developer clouded the attorney's judgment. The developer's team would fly into Ft. Lauderdale from Chicago. A total of five meetings were held at a third party's office provided by the Chicago firm. The prospective buyer never questioned the attorney's asking price. It seemed a given. There were difficulties to overcome regarding zoning, new roads and density but by the third meeting the language handling these issues was crafted and only the signature from an agent in Chicago was needed along with a cashier's check for the down payment. The fourth meeting produced the needed signer, but he brought a company check. At the fifth meeting the cashier's check was brought but the needed agent was missing. It was explained that he had already boarded the company plane in Chicago with his wife who suddenly suffered a kidney attack and they had to abort their flight. There was no sixth meeting. It was learned later that the Chicago firm bought a comparable site from a Boca Raton seller that they were also negotiating with during these visits to Florida.*

Mock Negotiations

Because bargaining sessions more likely resemble a tennis match than a golf game one cannot easily plan future moves. There are several common approaches used to train the reflexes of professional negotiators. One common type occurs in a industry classroom, with the participants broken into groups of four, two negotiating against another pair. Assume for example, that the class has 28 participants. That is seven sets of four "pretend" negotiators, two to each side: two buyers and two sellers. Each side is given a set of "facts." The seller's fact pattern is different from the buyer's on some points but similar on others. The parties are instructed to carry out their assignment and reach a settlement or deadlock within a stated time. Six sets of four retire to "breakout rooms" for these private bargaining sessions. The instructor then wanders among them and observes and notes certain behavior of the actors. Meanwhile, the seventh set is also segregated from the others and is making preparations to attempt to bargain in front of the others when they have finished their task. This seventh set of four is called "role players." Frequently "big mouths" are selected as role players for two reasons: so the others can hear the dialogue and because they might be less likely to suffer undue embarrassment should they blunder in public. Once the seven sets have privately given the instructor their results the role players begin to negotiate the same set of facts as the others in front of the entire group. When the role players finish their assignment considerable learning is about to begin because this phase is the "critique session." Here the parties who have bargained privately now question the moves of the role players. The answers and byplay can be so valuable that those who have a wish to obtain insight into human behavior and their own practices can be richly rewarded. The instructor then picks on the seven sets with such questions as "what was your aspiration point when you began," to "why did you say "split the difference" at the point where the other was about to make a concession?"

EXAMPLE   *Such sessions reveal behavior of both experienced and inexperienced bargainers. Many are surprised to learn that in the heat of the session they have made questionable moves: got angry when baited, suggested "we would like a long term relationship" when their assignment called for a one shot deal, lied when asked a question about their firm, used corny language like "that's like comparing apples and oranges," or "that is not even a drop in the bucket."*

Monetary Increment Game   See Concession Behavior

Monkey On Back   See Transference

Multiple Choice Questions

The old sales pitch, "Sir, will you be taking the blue or brown suit, or both," is a multiple choice question without a "none of the above" answer included. Those using the multiple choice questions when making presentations are placing their confidence in the value of setting premises. They are sometimes described as "Yessable Questions" (which see).

EXAMPLE   *"We can offer you a price of $68 a unit at our dock, $70 delivered to your Houston warehouse, or $71 delivered to your Fort Worth plant. We have enough units in stock to meet the order quantity you mentioned. Which works best for you?"*

Negative Qualities

Recitation of negative qualities in the other party's position or the qualities of the other party's products or services is an attempt to lower the expectations of the other party. This is not a tactic; rather it is a straightforward action and can be very effective if it is based on facts.

EXAMPLE   *Duncan is a patient negotiator and believes that his patience will be rewarded if he lets the Martin Company's negotiator boast about Martin's product quality, their excellent reputation for delivery, their generous credit terms, and so forth and so forth. As he listens to these grandiose claims he compares them with factual information he has gathered about Martin's actual performance. When Martin's negotiator finally "winds down" Duncan politely torpedoes most of Martin's claims with an accurate recital of Martin's shortcomings. The effect on Martin's negotiator is predictable, but if Duncan is wise he will not "rub it in," but rather will simply proceed with the negotiation from what has now become a position of strength for him.*

Negotiable Contracts

Professional contractors in many industries acknowledge that their firms actually negotiate less than 10% of their contracts. From a practical view point extensive negotiation effort is normally not worth the time and effort expended despite the fact that (marginally) better contracts might be made. However, extended negotiation conduct may be engaged in so as to send a message, rather than to achieve an immediate financial goal.

EXAMPLE   *Printing expense for Chesapeake-Dawson has never been a high priority in executive concerns. It has been convenient to deal with an old line supplier despite the rather rigid pricing quotes practiced by Old Line. At a luncheon honoring her the President of Chesapeake overheard a remark that disturbed her. The sales representative for Old Line was heard to say to another business person, "No, we set fair prices. We value our customers. If they don't trust us to be fair then we would rather not deal with them." Hearing these comments, the President had two thoughts: first, she did not want other firms believing that their view was the final determination in dealing*

with Chesapeake and, second, she has always been suspicious of negotiators who use the term "fair." Following the luncheon she scheduled a meeting with her Purchasing Manager.

Negotiation Dance

While the give and take in the dickering state resembles a tennis match, some academics have written it up as a "dance." This is particularly appropriate when specific terms are being discussed. Minor concessions are made, tentative offers are put forth, responses are given, and the dance goes on with, hopefully, progress being made with each set of steps. This is probably a good way to keep one's perspective so that successive comments made by the other are properly characterized as tentative, not excessively serious, and not likely final until agreement is at hand. To an observer the dance steps will appear to be somewhat intricate as two different tunes are being played at once.

EXAMPLE   *Most suppliers want to know how many units the buyer intends to buy. Disguising the quantity allows the buyer some negotiation movement. On the seller's side the mantra is words like "units," "production runs," "costs of gearing up" and so on, terms which the buyer wishes to avoid. Assume the buyer intends to purchase 200 units. The seller asks, "How many do you need? "What is your price for 10?" queries the buyer not answering the question. The seller begins the dance and begins to sway with, "10 only, well that would be $300 per unit." "What" screams (note the "Flinch,") that is outrageous; even in the best times you never got more than $160." "Ah," smoothly counters the seller, "You're so right, but that is for a production run of five hundred or more." The dance now gets slowly more serious as they deftly waltz quantities and dollars around the negotiation floor.*

Negotiation "Experts"

Early popular writers include Gerald I. Nierenberg, Chester L. Karrass and others. From academe, professors of psychology, management, mathematics, linguistics, decision theory and other fields wrote in scientific journals using both experiments and formulae to explain the subtle and practical aspects of management conflict. Seminar leaders are those professionals from both groups who are used in industry. This group of contributors to negotiation theory and practice have moved the discipline to a rather sophisticated state in the short 40 years that negotiation theory and practice have been formally treated. Practically, however, the day-to-day contractor must worry about applying theory in an environment called "human behavior." Generalizations are helpful, but in the heat of a session or sessions marshaling such gems tends to be quite difficult. Yet, an awareness of the many common practices called tactics, plus an appreciation of concession behavior and the like, will surely sharpen the practitioner as he or she practices the art of negotiation.

EXAMPLE   *Marcia loved two negotiation books. The principles were quite impressive and the anecdotes supporting their presentation were very entertaining. She found quickly in her own sessions, however, that it works best for her if she is aware of certain types of conduct rather than trying to carry out only preconceived tactics. She is learning the lesson that her active mind can assimilate much information, so she "loads the gun," relying on her mind to come to her rescue when certain "cues" pop up from the other side. The other day, for instance, she recognized the reason for her displeasure with a prospective contractor. He kept forgetting to bring in the cost figures needed to finalize the deal. Was she being treated to the missing man maneuver? It was time to find out.*

Negotiation Goals   See Preparation

Nibbling   See Also Freebies

Nibbling and Freebies both refer to the practice of obtaining "minor goodies" from a contractor. Freebies are items obtained when the whole negotiation is assumed by the other party to be a done deal. Nibbling, on the other hand, is the practice of taking tiny bites during the negotiation. A nibble is a request for slight change in a term the parties have just agreed upon. Such bites have value to the nibbler and are chosen to cost the other party very little. When a negotiator realizes he or she has run

into a nibbler, there are several alternatives available for handling the situation. First, if the negotiation is truly going well, let the nibbler get away with it; a happy nibbler may be easy to deal with. However, if the nibbler is a hard negotiator whose nibbles are starting to sting, the nibblee will likely want to put a stop to it by simply saying no.

EXAMPLE   *"Okay, Mike, that's 15 gallons of lubricant. Uh, couldn't we make that 16?" "I'm glad we're agreed on 6.1% interest Mary, but, ah, why not round it to an even 6%." "A nine percent return allowance sounds just fine and it's acceptable. But, come to think of it, you know, ten percent would be just as reasonable." And so forth.*

Nonnegotiable Items

As old as the hills is the aggressive announcement by a bargainer that such and such "is nonnegotiable." The other party must now test the integrity of this announcement. The test could be to ignore the statement and proceed with the business at hand or, alternatively, meet it head on. If the latter, one might want to determine whether the basis for the position applies to the prospective contract. Simply, it may well be that the speaker has misunderstood the significance of this obstacle. But, if the item truly seems to be nonnegotiable, whether warranted or not, it is not helpful to put it aside; it must be dealt with or accepted.

EXAMPLE   *The frontal attack: "We looked at your form contract. I will tell you right now that my firm does not look kindly on 'termination clauses.' In fact, I am going over my boss's head even to talk to you if indeed you are going to insist on such a clause." The object of this aggressive remark inwardly hears several possible sounds here. One, is this an attempt to dominate the session before we even begin? Two, why should that clause cause difficulty for them? Why do they anticipate that our form contract is carved in stone? What can I do to get around this point if we are to get the traditional protection this clause allows us in this kind of deal?*

Objective Criteria

Positional bargaining, and other forms of soft bargaining accommodate the introduction of objective criteria to lead the way to a successful negotiation. Objective criteria could include delivery schedules, production specifications, cost analysis and the like. If parties can point to facts or quasi-facts as determinants they may avoid the traditional bickering so common to hard bargaining. Nevertheless the identification of such criteria and the relative values to be placed on their presence may still require some form of hard bargaining skills.

EXAMPLE   *"All we need from you is the power tolerances for your machines, your cost figures submitted to an independent accountant, and the invoices for the last five sales of these units. The results of these measures will determine whether we can both use them to agree to a price at which we would pay a premium of 5% over the averages of these past five sales." Although it is usually more technical than the above illustrates, positional bargaining distinguishes itself by allowing objective criteria to substitute for the "games" occurring in the usual bargaining session. However, note that the party setting out the criteria by which he will pay a 5% premium is using a hard bargaining approach.*

Obstinacy

This is another term for bull-headedness. There is a large number of aggressive individuals whose nature seems inclined to the confrontational. One may assume that they were hired for that inclination or that such behavior is tolerated for the company's own reasons. Unfortunately, the negotiation literature suggests that obstinate persons do not fare poorly in negotiation. It may well be that a particular industry or field is used to that culture. Civility in the face of apparent inflexibility does well in courtrooms where third parties, the jurors, as a rule react negatively to bullies. Bargaining, however, has no third party referee and the only audience the bully is playing to is the opposition whom he or she hopes to intimidate.

EXAMPLE   *Typical obstinacy is illustrated by such statements as "That issue is not negotiable. That term (or price) might be high but it's fair. I've offered these terms for years and this is the first time someone has questioned this industry custom. You'll just have to accept what I say because I'm right."*

Open Price

There are several meanings to this term. From a non-technical view it refers to a price to be set by the "market," usually at time and place of performance. Market price is of course a product of industry averages, a fairly fluid term. Legally the meaning is quite precise, particularly when dealing in sales of personal property (goods), but setting it is neither easy or inexpensive. Under the Uniform Commercial Code, Section 2-305, if the parties left the price for later agreement, the price is a "reasonable" one at time and place of delivery. This means that only a trial court (or arbitrator if applicable) could determine what is "reasonable" after hearing evidence of what a willing buyer and seller might pay.

EXAMPLE   *"Ok, it is agreed, we are all reasonable people here. We need the machine. Your cost figures are not in but we have a deal and we are confident you will treat us fairly." This is an open price situation. Unless the parties can agree on a figure a court will settle the issue. Despite the uncertainty of a material term, the price, a contract was formed under the UCC.*

Opening Statements

If there was ever a place for intelligence, imagination and dedication to the challenges of a negotiation it surely would be in the content and delivery of the opening statements. The opportunity to set the stage is unique, or as the saying goes, "you never get a second chance to make a first impression." For those interested in agenda setting, premises, and the lowering of expectations, for examples, the opening dialogue can provide the platform for these objectives. The difficulty is that one must know the foreign territory, i.e., the opponent. Where prior investigation is not conducted, or where it is difficult, negotiators rely on their standard inclinations. Here, a benign opening, appropriate to the negotiator's personality and industry culture is called for; a piece of business he or she has felt does little damage when fishing in unknown waters.

EXAMPLE   *Hi, Harry! Did you see in the latest Industry Newsletter the article saying that OSHA is going to relax some of their dumber regulations? That's one piece of good news for both of us. And did you see in the paper, the airlines are going to cut their fares five percent? I know we both do a lot of company travel and that should help both our budgets. Speaking of airlines, I think I set a record last week—six flights and they were all on time for a change. Well, will it be just us, or will one of your engineering people be sitting in?"*

Opportunity Cost

Actually, the term "opportunity *cost*" is misleading. It is usually a matter of deciding which course of action will yield better results than would alternative courses of action. And, a decision to proceed in one way frequently forecloses or narrows a firm's opportunity to pursue other paths of action. Contracting with one vendor from among half a dozen possible suppliers illustrates an opportunity cost decision, as would be the case of a negotiator during a bargaining session electing to trade off a less desirable term for a more desirable one.

EXAMPLE *Echo Industries had a long-term relationship with Bolt Supply. The natural effects of such an association were beginning to appear. Better terms were not being offered by Bolt and the firm's negotiator enjoyed some bonding with Echo's people. As matters stood, Bolt had clearly become a bad choice with a negative opportunity cost for Echo. Echo's senior management finally woke up and instructed its negotiator to notify Bolt that the party was over. Unless Bolt promptly began offering better terms Echo would negotiate with other suppliers.*

Options

The term "option" in negotiation does not refer to a legal option but rather to the array of possible moves a bargainer has available when dealing with the other party. [A legal option is an enforceable promise by one that another may, but need not, exercise.] Sometimes negotiation preparation reveals that there appears to be no alternative but to contract with a party on such terms as the other may impose. Here, the advice (hope) is to create alternatives, or at least give the appearance to the other side that you do have choices, that you do have options. Imagination and creativity are at a premium in such situations as is a willingness to take a rational risk.

EXAMPLE   *In the course of a long relationship Barrowe & Co. had placed themselves in the unenviable position of having relied on Tailor Feed who bought 70% of one of their major products. They had accommodated this buyer in many ways so that a substantial part of this product's manufacturing process was geared to serve Tailor. This is analogous to the single source situation. (Which see). Here, imaginative alternatives must be pursued, including the riskiest of all, the possibility of a "deadlock" should Tailor's terms be too onerous. Modifying the risk would be the point that there might be no other vendor who could supply Tailor's substantial needs on short notice. Barrowe's negotiator might even be able to convince Tailor that it is Tailor that has a problem, not Echo.*

Partners Theory

In attempting to make business a friendly endeavor some bargainers take the word "partner" as the elixir that transforms an anxious and serious encounter into a love feast. Business negotiators should realize that casual use of the word partner is potentially dangerous. Those who practice soft bargaining, to which partners theory is closely allied, should understand that partner is an ancient legal term. In fact it is reported that there are more legal partnerships in the United States than any other form of business association. The legal definition of a "partnership" is "an association of two or more persons to carry on as co-owners of a business for profit."

EXAMPLE   *Nettleton is quite careless with terms. He is a hale fellow well met and is non judgmental of others. He hope others are as easy going. He runs a print shop with Lisa, his sister-in-law. They incorporated the business but he still introduces Lisa as his "partner in the business." This is risky behavior if he is relying on the protection of the corporate form. He treats the supplier of his paper as a "partner" when they dicker over prices and delivery. "We are in this together Jasper," he would say, "If you don't treat us right you don't succeed." While experienced bargainers should not take the partner ploy seriously, any reference suggesting such a relationship should not be entertained.*

Patience

One does not have to be brilliant, well trained or even old to practice patience in negotiation. However, this trait is one of the most difficult to possess. Patience in negotiation includes the ability to restrain the busy tongue and quick harsh judgments, and instead practice that rare facility of "suffering fools." Many tactics used in bargaining need this handmaiden.

EXAMPLE   *Gloria is seemingly unflappable. But don't ask to see her blood pressure reading. Gloria never interrupts a presentation and always displays a neutral countenance. She found early in life that a fair percentage of her clients love to posture; and she lets them. She believes in the time investment tactic, and found that her patience is the "hard currency" by which she extends the bargaining session to her advantage.*

Patters And Nudgers

Touching has become a "touchy subject" today in legal circles. The practice of the stereotypical car salesperson placing his arm on another's back with the accompanying promise "to fix you up with a great little car," while still experienced in business, tends to identify a less than subtle operator. But what does this aggressive behavior tell the negotiator? Traditionally such conduct has been interpreted as the deportment of an outgoing personality who, by innuendo, is suggesting his or her dominance in the meeting.

EXAMPLE   *Harold is a toucher, he has a great smile, and "avuncu-*
           lar" is his middle name. He uses the nudge as an invita-
           tion to have you join in agreement over a joke, principle,
           or judgment. It is difficult to see how interpreting this
           conduct could play a role in the bargaining session. It is
           merely, to some, an irritating habit. To the extent, how-
           ever, that it undermines the confidence of the party
           nudged or patted, it qualifies as a tactic.

Performance Specification

Parties frequently negotiate for a degree of "quality" expected and promised by the parties. Quality in this sense deals with the specifications of the product or service. At its optimum a buyer

of a product or service would naturally desire that the product or service will achieve the buyer's needs. However, a promise to provide performance is usually quite expensive to the buyer. Simply illustrated, a manufacturer may be willing to guarantee or warrant that its "#3 two-inch steel bolt" meets industry specifications (ASTM). Such a commitment identifies a "technical specification." But if the manufacturer is asked to promise that four of them would securely hold a particular model of radar device against wind-forces up to 120 mph there will be hesitation by an experienced negotiator. This last request is a request for a "performance specification."

EXAMPLE   *The parties were negotiating for the purchase and sale of a combustion engine. The seller had a number of models at different prices. The buyer needed a device capable of delivering sufficient power to run their #520 Lifter." Each model was engraved by the seller with its warranted output and other specifications. These, if conveyed to the buyer, are express warranties and would be consistent with what is called a "technical specification," that is data which stands by itself without promise of any particular application. The seller's price for a model that would achieve a buyer's objective for a particular use, a "performance specification,"will usually be a highly negotiated one. In such a case, observe the greater risk and undertaking by the seller. If willing to so commit, the seller will attempt to get big bucks for this performance warranty.*

Personalization

Whether Leo Durocher ever actually said "nice guys finish last" is open to question but that is the common truth of the statement under many circumstances, and these include negotiation. Business is business and personal problems are personal

problems, or so goes the logic. Yet this exemplary statement is frequently denied by practitioners with behavior that might be called personalization or personal pleas. This may involve new business or old relationships. Either case deserves little respect. First, it is clearly used to gain sympathy and second, it may be employed as a bargaining chip or tactic.

EXAMPLE   *"Charlene, this is the first time we've met, but I'm asking you to give me a good price here, we are restructuring and my position is under review and I am hanging on to my job with my fingernails!" This plea, of questionable ethics, may accompany an express or implied promise of a "payback" in the future. Realists are skeptical here, believing gratitude is a weak motive for behavior even where the party can assist in the future. And, in this example, even if Charlene goes along with the plea, the pleader may lose his job anyway and a payback would never materialize.*

It was 4:30 in the afternoon and the deal was nearly set, but the parties were still $2 apart on price, the buyer at $37 and the sales rep at $39. The buyer had known the sales rep for several years; he was a nice fellow and always showed the latest pictures of his wife and kids. He said, "Look, I've got a 5:30 plane. If I miss it I'm stuck here overnight. How about we close this out at $38?" The buyer knew that the 5:30 plane was the last one to st. Louis that day, but should reject the rep's offer, saying, "Thirty-nine is too much. My offer is thirty-seven and that's as high as I will go." If the seller has time-trapped himself that is his problem, not the buyer's. It is worth noting that the rep's plea combines personalization and the "split the difference" tactic (which see).

Persuasive Personality

It is difficult to specify what qualities make some persons able to alter the viewpoint or behavior of others. But it does appear that a persuader may only be effective, or at least more effective, in his own his environment and, secondly, the "persuader" must have an optimistic view of the outcome when dealing with others.

EXAMPLE   *Campbell was a claims specialist who came on strong to most people. He smiled, was a bit gauche, but was outgoing and to a certain extent was tolerated. He always appeared very sure of himself and was quite successful in getting insurance claims settled favorably for his clients. He specialized in modest claims which he privately characterized as "easy for the companies to settle," and habitually referred large claims to a law firm in his city. No one would have described Campbell as having a smooth personality, yet within his milieu he was a persuasive personality.*

Positional Bargaining

Negotiators practice hardball when they announce seemingly fixed positions that are considerable distances from each other. This is considered a hard bargaining approach and is used in those situations where the practice is common, as in union-management disputes, or in other environments where the parties by their particular tradition tend to begin far apart. While considered to be understandably detrimental to moving easily and quickly to settlement, it is still widely practiced.

EXAMPLE   *At one time if a bank's debtor was in arrears the poor unfortunate would come to the bank on bended knee. Today, many firms and nations owe very large sums to banks, and when the banks attempt to collect, the debtors now resist and take strong positions against the bank. The bank calls this bank-debtor negotiation by the innocuous name "work out." The bank demands its back interest and resumption of repayment of principal. The debtor arrogantly insists on waiver of all past interest and a "restructure of the principal amount." Truly, these parties are about to practice positional bargaining.*

Posturing

Concepts such as the "time investment theory"(which see) contribute to the negotiation patterns in the United States and many other nations. This means that it is sometimes helpful for a party to induce the other to invest some time in the encounter. The inducement might include some behavior that is play acting. Secondly, parties normally do not get down to business without some attempt to observe the normal amenities of social discourse, even Americans who are reputed to be too brusque in business dealings. Thirdly, acting can set up some favorable "premises" (which see). Fourth, how else to size up the other side except without testing some reactions by a "bit of business?" And finally there are moments in some sessions in which some dramatics might be summoned by one of the parties. All of these objectives may call for some posturing.

EXAMPLE   *Posturing includes: the good cop- bad cop scenario, vocal outrage when a term is offered by the other side (flinch), apparent disinterest in dealing with the other side, telling time-wasting anecdotes, asking for information likely to take some time for the other party to get, taking frequent (long) breaks for one reason or another, taking an extended lunch hour, and so forth. Clearly, there will be a limit on how much of such conduct the "posturee" will tolerate, and the wise negotiator will not press his or her luck.*

Power, Impression Of

It is not uncommon for parties to admit to shyness and a fear that others may be more powerful than they. This mind set can be avoided by recognizing that fancy trappings are common vehicles by which parties attempt to intimidate. When faced with indicia of intimidation it is necessary to examine their relevancy to the negotiation.

EXAMPLE   *"Yes, we want to buy from you, but if we cannot get a reasonable deal we are prepared to buy out Sansone (the competitor) and become our own supplier" If this is a real possibility, it conveys a true impression of power. However, a beautiful conference room, complete with fancy audiovisual equipment, computerized displays, and executive chairs around a large mahogany table is simply ostentatious display irrelevant to any question of negotiating power.*

Precedent

Courts in the United States and England pay homage to precedent (the basis for the doctrine called **stare decisis**) when they examine like cases in the past to settle controversies before them. It is a powerful doctrine and its influence carries over into other parts of business life. Bargainers frequently practice this doctrine to justify their postion. It is up to the other party to make two points in rebuffing a precedent. First, the business table is not a court bench and, secondly, one may distinguish the present situation from the earlier experience.

EXAMPLE   *"Madeleine, your form contract has been used by us without objection for the past 3 years and its 90-day notice of termination clause has up until now worked well for both of us. However, our new operations will involve a longer break-in period, so our requested change to a 190-day termination notice clause is an appropriate adjustment."*

Premises

The old saying "You are begging the question" refers to premises. It originally meant the following: "You, like a beggar, come to me and ask that I grant the first favorable premise to you." In negotiation, a party who can establish a favorable point materially advances his interest. A seller's statement that "company policy forbids liquidated damage clauses in our contracts" is the speaker's explicit attempt to establish a favorable premise. One must be careful to recognize these attempts, as once a premise is established early it is quite difficult to dislodge it later.

EXAMPLE   *Experienced negotiators know that they will often have to deal with an attempt to establish a premise offered by the other party. Similar to a baseball shortstop fielding a grounder and throwing the batter out at first base, our negotiator must "field the offered premise" and dispose of it. Many effective responses are available, such as: "Knock it off Eddie. You know that's nonsense." or "What a wonderful idea. Let me tell you our fairy tale and we'll trade." or "If that's a joke, I didn't get the punch line." And so forth. The objective is to get the premise off the table and on the floor where it can be stepped on.*

Preparation

The vague charge of "you must prepare" to a negotiator or a team of negotiators needs more specificity. General instructions such as "get a good deal" or "don't make a bad one" are unhelpful. Because not all the facts or contentions to be raised by the other side are known, the superior formulating the charge must select appropriate language in setting objectives. The bargainers must actually memorize certain company and industry data so that in the heat of the session such material comes handily, and just as importantly, convincingly. Team members must be particularly careful in their preparation in order that they stay on the same page. Further, the play must have some tentative opening, as well as closing moves. Finally, the participants must be conscious of certain traditional behavior patterns that will play out in nearly all negotiations. They include trade offs (which see) concession behavior, the monetary increment game (which see) and that corny practice of split the difference (which see).

EXAMPLE   *Lucille is quite brilliant but admits that she doesn't always think quickly on her feet. She is usually well prepared to come up with factual data without hesitation. But, despite having fully absorbed her own company's data and the opponent's likely positions and situation, she has been caught more than once at a critical moment when that trite thrust, "let's split the difference," is tossed on the table by the other party. She did anticipate the possibility, but what has hurt her is her failure to be disciplined in her concession behavior. To improve her negotiating skills she must learn to control her responses to the other party's tactics.*

Price Increases

The announcement of a price increase is viewed as a hostile act, whether such an increase is justified or not. The recipient of this news is unhappy and does not take kindly to explanations that outside forces or situations force a party to raise prices. Such announcement can be assigned to the category of a tactic for any number of reasons:

EXAMPLE   *"Our supplier raised the price of copper." [What is being said: Obviously, you the buyer must pay for this, we don't intend to]. "We just can't make a profit on this sale unless we raise the price." [What is being said: Ok, so we run a bad ship, but with the personnel and shop we have this is the only way we can make a profit, and we aren't going to take the licking] "This increase is in line with industry trends" [What is being said: What a windfall for us, we still have inventory at lower costs, great break] "I understand you are concerned but the bosses have instructed me quite clearly on this." [What may be happening: We know our competitors are raising their prices too, so you won't get a better deal elsewhere.]*

Principled Negotiation

The adoption of this method tests the parties' ability to be forthcoming as to both their objectives and resources. Each party addresses the needs and capabilities of the other having determined that unless these aspects are addressed and satisfied the deal would not be successful for both. It has been offered that "objective criteria" for evaluating each other's proposals is a major premise in this type of bargaining.

EXAMPLE   *Both companies have determined that an unsuccessful performance of their proposed contract could have dire consequences for each. They agree to exchange confidential information regarding delivery, quality, cost figures, production data, financial resources and marketing information concerning the objectives of each party. Further, it is agreed that such factors will drive the terms of their finished agreement.*

Problem Solving

This is the name given to a form of soft bargaining. In the abstract, at least, the approach requires both parties to exchange truthful information about needs and priorities and then search for mutually satisfying alternatives. The difficulty in obeying these criteria is that while satisfactory results on both sides is an announced goal the reality is common that both parties may have to some extent conflicting needs.

EXAMPLE   *Following the example given above [Principled Negotiation] assume that both parties start out with genuine intent to negotiate in that fashion. But, it turns out that despite their intentions two problems have appeared: the buyer believes it is absolutely necessary that there be a six-year warranty on these machines and, further, that the seller maintain the dies necessary for making replacement parts for twelve years. The seller struggles with the problems posed by these requirements and finally concludes that they would impose much too great a burden. The buyer's engineering and production people maintain that their warranty and parts replacement requirements are necessary for this model of machine. Clearly, it is going take some serious thought and innovation to solve this problem which is real for both parties.*

Puffing

In old case law "puffing" was a judgment rendered about favorable statements about products which were not actionable at law against the speaker. Boasts that "it is the finest on the market," or "an excellent buy" are examples of puffing. Perhaps it gained such immunity from the adage "let the

buyer beware" in purchasing products, a byproduct taken from the lesson taught through the experience that the buyer needs a hundred eyes, the seller not one. Negotiators are supposed to be immune to favorable statements about products or services one wishes to peddle to them. What both the legal eagle and the bargainer must look for are statements about products or services that have concrete meaning. It is here the negotiator takes interest and ties the speaker to his or her words.

EXAMPLE   *"Will this valve work for your purposes? You bet your life it will, this is state of art (puffing) and will take care of the problem you describe." This comment, in its entirety is not puffing but a promise (warranty) that the valve will perform the task the buyer described. Accordingly, while the words "state of the art" are puffing, the added comment that "this . . . will take care of the problem you describe" is a legally enforceable promise.*

Put Downs

A negotiator may use a "put down" for the perfectly reasonable purpose of lowering the expectations of the other party. The difficulty is that put downs can strongly offend the other party. But, if one chooses to do so, there are subtleties of technique that operate nicely to avoid serious offense. In this regard, the negotiator's own experience usually provides areas of opportunity. The test is to use these in an ethical and professional manner. That is not always easy, nor is it always successful.

EXAMPLE   *Signing Sam has been selling cars for 30 years. His bluff manner usually intimidates. Sam's favorite practice is to look at a prospective used car trade-in and find some fault with it. "Darn, I could have sold this baby yesterday if the dashboard had been better protected against the sun. It's funny how a little thing like that turns off a buyer." Another salesperson, Sympathy Sue, uses the put down by being sorry for "unlucky" customers. "Your model had great trade-in value six months ago, but since then articles about low-gas-mileage cars like yours have given us trouble. We usually don't try to resell them here. We send them to a wholesaler at a reduced price." A savvy customer would spot both approaches as tactics.*

Questions

Carefully constructed and discreetly delivered, use questions is considered an effective negotiation tool. "Would you tell me more so that I can understand that point better," if uttered with the right tone is a standard in negotiation banter. Oddly, questions can be smooth vehicles but they also are confrontational when delivered aggressively or when the substance of the question itself is insulting, and counterproductive.

EXAMPLE *"Let me understand this, you are offering a product you won't warrant more than a year and asking a price 12% over your competitors. Why should we consider this a serious offer?" Or more likely, safer questions such as: "What would be the first part of the project?" "What is the least relevant aspect of this product?" "What would your customers say if I asked about your firm?" "Is there a particular aspect of this deal that is more important to you? "*

Quick Negotiations

It is a sad commentary that the laudable goal of direct and relevant bargaining is not practiced in the United States, or many other places as well. It may be a cultural trait which prevents parties from quickly getting down to the main business. Yet, the theorists are probably correct when they offer that quick negotiations tend to result in big winners and big losers.

EXAMPLE   *In a recent mock negotiation program eight teams of four bargainers struck a deal, none deadlocked. The simple fact pattern used by the mock negotiators is constructed to take from 30 to 40 minutes to settle. One of the teams used only 10 minutes to reach agreement. The others used up most of the allotted time. The buyers in the first-to-finish group were the big winners. The sellers agreed to the lowest price, selling their product at 25% less than the average price of the other sellers in the program. The buyers of course won the mock negotiation contest with this best deal.*

Quick Quote

Asking for a quick quote can jump start a negotiation and thus avoid wasting time, so goes a particular theory. And, experienced debaters and bargainers learn quickly the benefits flowing from a quick acceptance, implied or explicit, of the first premise. Quick quote requests that catch the other side unprepared can result in a favorable premise being established by the questioner. The potential responder should have an inventory of safe statements when a "quick quote request" is made.

EXAMPLE   *"I understand that we are a bit premature here, but look-*
ing at our budget I am interested in a quick quote based
on what I have told you." Should the party choose to
answer, the "quote" statement might be tailored to the
particular industry or circumstances. Such might sound
like this: "It sounds like it would run about X Dollars,
provided our three conditions are met." or "I hate to tell
you, but it could run as high as X dollars unless there are
some features that you would be willing to exclude from
the requirement." It is being prepared for the question
that is important, as such homework allows for fabrica-
tion of an imaginative and relevant response.

Real Estate Contract

Usually, negotiating for the purchase and sale of real estate has a
different setting and includes experts not generally found in
many sessions. Unfortunately, in the United States a transaction
in real estate, whatever its dollar value, is an expensive and time
consuming adventure. There are "standard" contract forms as
bases from which the parties dicker over numerous delicate and
material terms. This is not to say that common negotiating techniques are not used; they are. Only that a real estate bargaining
session is a production number in this country and that the
training in this field includes knowledge of the subtleties of real
property commitments and consequences.

EXAMPLE   *Adler Products need additional space. Next door is an*
old (70 years) dry-cleaning establishment where the
owner has died and her family will not carry on the busi-
ness. To buy the land, space on earth, the parties must
enter into a real estate purchase and sale agreement. The
negotiator is not looking at an entirely clean deal. It is
true a title search will check the ownership of the seller
negotiator and claims others have on the property but

there are some considerations not so evident. Will the zoning allow Adler to use it as it intends? Will there be an EPA issue? Simply, this was a dry-cleaning establishment. How many hazardous chemicals made their way into the ground during the past 70 years? A provision in the contract here might be difficult but without such assurance of clean ground the issue is a deal breaker. More than any other type of contract real estate transactions have performance problems, all conditioned on the multiple terms in the contract.

Real Reason

Like umbrella issues (which see) the ground which supports another's position or demand is sometimes hidden. Yet, while a bargainer might give "reasons" for a particular price, delivery, or whatever, the pivotal justification is frequently unrevealed. In parenting, for example, the experts warn of giving secondary reasons for a decision or principle. "The reason you can't go to

the party is that it is raining." The counter argument:."But his father is driving." The real reason is that you just don't want her going with that boy, period. Unless one is prepared to reveal the real reason, secondary or tertiary reasons only invite debate and cause difficulties as well as leaving one open to a charge of deceit. A Supreme Court justice in talking about reasons and finality was quoted as saying, "My answer is no, and so that you know it is final I give you no reasons." In negotiating it is not useful to expose false presentations where the point may not be relevant to the negotiation, but there are times when giving false reasons opens a bargainer to fatal attack.

EXAMPLE   *The well-known actress Raquel Welch was fired during the filming of* Cannery Row *by the MGM Studio. The studio had the right to terminate her services at any time during the filming without giving any reason, provided it paid her $250,000 contract. Rather than simply terminating her services and paying off her contract, the studio publicly gave out a number of "reasons" for firing her which were found not to be true, reasons which damaged her professional reputation in the film industry. Ms. Welch sued the studio for slander and was ultimately awarded $5,000,000 in punitive damages. The studio would have done well to follow the Supreme Court justice's example noted above.*

Reservation Price   See Resistance Point

Resistance Point

In planning a negotiation is there an absolute position beyond which one will not deal? Writers on the subject express varied opinions regarding when and how this position should be revealed. For example, an early notification of this point may

destroy the effectiveness of one's concession behavior. It could be interpreted as a tactical synonym for the "non negotiable" ploy, usually of questionable worth except against the naive. What writers do not instruct on is how this resistance point is calculated. For sellers, for instance, cost, market conditions, the financial position of the company, cash flow, a message to the industry that they wish to deliver, or just plain stubbornness might contribute to the setting of this position. The determination of the resistance point is usually made at a higher managerial level than that of the operating negotiator.

EXAMPLE   *Alberta had clear instructions that under no circumstances was she to settle for less than $32,500. However, the arguments the other side made were compelling. The market was very competitive as supply was increasing and her company was no longer considered the premier in its field. This last possibility came as a shock to her because management had stressed this point. No deal was reached and research tracked the "resistance point" figure to a vow made by the vice president in sales who believed that such a weakness in price made the company "just another supplier." Avoiding being perceived as such was important to "management."*

Restating Positions

A speaker's practice of restating the other party's contention, argument or offer can instruct the other in several ways. First, if the content is correct the restater has indeed listened to the material aspects of the presentation. Second, it gives the hearer an opportunity to understand the matter as expressed by another, and, if the speaker is human, hearing it delivered with tone or nuances that might give the original speaker some pause. The drill can assist an effective negotiator.

EXAMPLE   *"Okay, let's see if I have this right. You can deliver my quantity and on the time schedule I need provided we make payment up front. And the reason you insist on prepayment is because quantity and time need financing?"*

Restricted Authority

Firms rarely give full discretion to their agents and the tactic, sometimes called "limited authority," recognizes this. The term means to describe the practice of those managers who unreasonably circumscribe their agent's power. Unreasonably in this context implies that the user has, by this instruction to its agent, exceeded the bounds of appropriate agency scope under the circumstances of the pending transaction or industry practice.

EXAMPLE   *The seller's agent was asked by a buyer about the nature of the warranty for the items in question. The agent apologetically replied that "only the home office has authority to determine the term of any warranty." Whether this is an attempted tactic or appropriate behavior depends on the nature of the industry or custom*

regarding certain products. For expensive airplane parts, landing gears, for instance, it could be an industry practice that the term of warranty is a matter left for later negotiations. However, in the normal course of affairs "cuteness" about a warranty issue suggests that a "bit of business" is being attempted. Experienced bargainers do not tolerate unreasonable assertions about lack of authority.

Risk Taking

When the subject of risk is raised the negotiator should remember that a ship in harbor is safe, but that is not what ships are built for. Risk averse behavior is generally not an asset in negotiation because it will, more often than not, result in costly concessions. However, an imprudent risk taker is essentially a gambler with an unwarranted overconfidence in expectations of success and a lack of appreciation for the intangibles and conflict dynamics that occur during negotiation. The example illustrates a proper approach to risk taking.

EXAMPLE *Lauren fits the stereotypical profile of a risk taker. She is enthusiastic, manages change both quickly and effortlessly, and believes that an optimistic nature is a great asset. In negotiation the action is more like tennis than golf. Each shot from the other sends a message which must be understood and acted upon. Prudent risk taking by Lauren requires an objective real-time estimate of the situation and an assessment of the probable result of any action contemplated by her. Prudent risks are calculated risks that are likely to succeed. They carry no guarantees, but as Damon Runyon said, "The race is not always to the swift nor the battle to the strong, but that's the way to bet."*

Role Playing

Role playing is a popular exercise in matters other than negotiation. In law, for example, pretend lawsuits are fashioned with members of the law firm and their witnesses going through a mock trial. Those so participating are role playing. So too with training sessions in negotiations.

EXAMPLE   *Those parties who take sides and play act in front of critics are role players. In mock negotiation training sessions the training provides the other participants a critical view of the dynamics of a bargaining session. To some trainers the role playing segment and the critique by the participants provide the most fruitful of lessons to those wishing to recognize their own behavior and thereby improve their negotiation skills.*

Satisfactory Negotiation

This term is used in two ways. First, those who stress the win-win approach to conflict management believe that each side should be satisfied with the session's outcome. In this context there are critics who argue that taking on the task of pleasing others is a bit patronizing when fashioning business contracts. Contracting is not a friendly endeavor despite some popular rhetoric to the contrary. A contract is serious business as it alters the legal relationship of the parties; the legal system, while punishing bad behavior such as fraud and overreaching, does not protect the dunce. Simply stated, the law recognizes that parties may make fools of themselves when contracting; bad bargains are legally enforceable. The second meaning of this phrase deals with the personal judgment negotiators express about their fashioned agreement after the session has ended. It is common folklore among negotiators that each side seems pleased at that time but a review of the deal by others often produces a different judgment.

EXAMPLE   *After a tiring session a deal has been made. Each party now reviews her instructions and finds that (1) she met the objectives set, or (2) came within a reasonable distance of them, or (3) has a good explanation to take back to her superiors. What frequently is missing in this self evaluation is the absence of the main point: did each party press their aspiration level properly or were they playing it safe? Professional satisfaction in this regard should mean that high aspirations were entertained and pressed during the session. Any lesser performance cannot be characterized as having produced a "satisfactory negotiation outcome."*

Secret Information

The problem with information, secret or otherwise, is that the possessor must have the discipline to properly incorporate this knowledge into the bargaining session. The temptation to capitalize on the material is great but the manner and timing of employment is not easy to fashion. Simply, most individuals are not born poker players with the patience and skill to use mind-changing information. Those studying behavior in this area suggest that without such patience and skill one is better off without secret information. They believe that uninformed bargainers usually begin with higher initial bids, take longer to reach agreement, and gain greater advantage in their bargaining than do informed bargainers.

EXAMPLE   *In a training session delivered to the personnel of a computer company a senior purchasing agent with 22 years of experience expressed cynicism over whether inside or secret information could actually hurt one in the session. One of the mock sessions had embedded in it a fact pattern that included information that was a secret weakness that the other side was bringing into the bargaining session. When the exercise was completed and the scores calculated, the senior's contract was found wanting, by himself. He expressed surprise to the instructor that he mishandled this advantage so poorly because it affected both his preparation and his aspiration level when the other side did not lay down and play dead when he crudely delivered the blow.*

Seller's Cost

Few would deny that the seller's "cost" to produce and deliver a service or product is relevant to the seller, but may not govern his actions. Cost is relevant to the buyer only if convinced that it has some bearing on the negotiation. A product or service may be offered by many sources and the cost figures (if known) of these different sources might play a role in the negotiation. However, why a particular party would offer an item or service at what the buyer believes is below the seller's cost raises several possibilities. Sellers sometimes bid to get some business, to sell goods destined for salvage, to keep a plant in operation, or to accommodate their other interests, making cost irrelevant. The adept buyer keeps these possibilities in mind.

EXAMPLE   *In a classic mock negotiation problem a seller is attempting to dispose of king-size mattress springs which were produced through an error in instructions from sales. Meanwhile, a mattress manufacturer, whose other plant also make springs is about to go on strike just when a sales campaign for king-size bed units is being launched. The manufacturer goes to the seller and, of course, has inside information: it knows the cost of manufacturing king-size springs. What the buyer doesn't know is that the seller is about ready to sell its king-size springs for salvage. A buyer who assumes that the "cost" in its own plant, or in others in the industry, is important at all times might miss the opportunity presented here. In mock sessions only the disciplined participant does not let the "seller's cost" (a figure which is likely to be close to its own cost) to unduly influence the session.*

Service Contract

While legalities of form, whether the agreement is oral or written, are not prime factors in much negotiation, the educated business person recognizes that the law takes a different view of oral agreements regarding goods, land or services (everything else). Simply, most oral agreements for the sale of goods or services require few, if any, formalities to make them qualify as binding contracts. [Land, i.e. space on earth, and those things (e.g., buildings).the law considers permanently attached to them is a different matter. Simply, in a bargaining session a final agreement over the sale of land will not be legally firm until documents are signed by both parties and lawyers or land specialists will be playing major roles.] Service contracts generally are binding at the negotiation table after a handshake or its equivalent. The only time this is not true is when the agreement to perform the service specifies a year or more (in most states) to fully complete the contract. Interestingly, the way courts look at the year provision permits performance for much longer periods depending on the phrasing of the agreement.

EXAMPLE   *Assume that a firm ordered a prime contractor to construct additional warehouse space for a contract price of $2 million. This is a contract calling for a service despite the fact it is on land and will involve considerable construction materials, i.e., personal property. The specifications were agreed upon for this building and it took 15 months to complete, but the parties had no restriction as to completion date, except that it be erected in a "timely manner". Because the parties did not explicitly specify a construction time of more than a year, a handshake at the bargaining table made this an enforceable oral contract.*

Silence

In one mock session a negotiation team leader instructed an inexperienced member to just listen to the other side while the team leader was out of the room. Upon return the leader found that new proposed terms from the other side were extremely favorable and were caused, apparently, by the other side's perception that the team was toughening its position by the member's lack of reaction to other terms. Silence can force others to fill the void. It is, however, a risky maneuver because to many persons silence implies consent or agreement. If this perception is incorrect the situation will become confused and the negotiation will have to get re-started from some previous point.

EXAMPLE   *A young lawyer was hired by a firm in which his superior was quite close mouthed. The superior was, seemingly, a pipe smoker. It was rarely lit but the superior frequently was attempting to ignite the tobacco. In between attempts the superior would converse with his opponent with such half phases as "Ahem," "Interesting" "But how . . ." "But why . . ." and other such unrevealing comments and questions. The young lawyer was amazed at the number of parties who were unable to handle this bit of business and would volunteer statements, answer questions, and the like. Truly, this was silence in action.*

Single Source

In commercial contracting good sources are sometimes at a premium. Present day buyers tend to look to fewer sources of supply of goods or services after first vetting eligible firms. A classic case of single source can be seen in government contracting for goods or services that are not off the shelf. Simply, the successful bidder in the construction of a rocket engine of certain technical and unique specifications sees a favorable future as a likely single source. This stereotype follows through in many items or services not as sophisticated as space age requirements. A single-source situation may arise because of a seller's patents, or very high capital costs of production equipment (i.e. entry barrier), or manufacturing expertise, etc. Where there is only one source, a single source, negotiating favorable terms is somewhat handicapped. Yet, all may not be lost.

EXAMPLE   *Kinnard Enterprises produced air conditioning systems requiring a part that was available only from Belland Company. Belland had a patent on this part and had become increasingly difficult to deal with in respect to price. Kinnard's people were frustrated. How could they deal with Belland on something like a level playing field instead of being price gouged? A Kinnard engineer suggested a variation on the "make or buy" concept: redesign the air conditioning system so it would no longer need Belland's part; this would involve a large one-time development cost but it could be done and it would solve the problem. At the next negotiating session, Kinnard's people made a blunt request for a price reduction on a take it or leave it basis. The Belland salespeople tried to figure out what was going on, but the Kinnard people were non-responsive; they merely repeated their price reduction demand and this time followed it with a one-hour deadline for agreement by Belland. Belland gave in as they wanted the sale even at the reduced price, but they didn't have a clue as to what had happened. Had they been bluffed? Had a competitor somehow gotten around Belland's patent? Or, what?*

Situational Power

Of all the fears of the bargainer the possibility of the presence of excessive power in the other predominates. There are several factors to consider when this fear arises. They include: is the fear warranted? is the other party aware of this advantage? are there some of one's own options that exist or can be created which would assist in the negotiation? The fear may be warranted in some situations, but the advice of an experienced car sales manager regarding the buyer's position should be heeded. This manager, having participated in and managed thousands of car sales advised the following: unless you have selected one other car at another dealer which you absolutely would take if the session before you does not work out, you are at a strong disadvantage. Options hold the key to negotiators who fear situational power on the other side even if they must creatively fashion them. If you don't, or can't, keep the other party unaware of the existence of the situational power he or she possesses. Your only savior is options.

EXAMPLE   *A lawyer for building contractors, with considerable experience with real estate, was in the market for a new home. He bought a new home and was asked the purchase price by a colleague. The lawyer responded and the colleague then asked what was the seller's list price. "The same," replied the lawyer. "What," he was asked, "with all your experience in this field you were unable to get a lower price?" "That's it," was the reply, "but you must understand the seller had secret information." "Really, what was this secret information that prevented you from doing a better negotiation job." "Easy," was the attorney's response, "the seller knew that we wanted this house."*

Sometimes situational power is created by the victim; it was in this case.

Slips Of The Tongue

Because some literally act as if bargaining is a combination of war and sport, tension causes some tongues to betray thoughts the other parties pick up on. In certain behavior patterns, such as the monetary increment game, a slip regarding a term, for example can drastically raise the expectations of the opponent. Team negotiations are particularly vulnerable to this misadventure. Unintended slips include other such misses as the exposure of company documents carelessly left for others to see and one-sided phone calls heard by the opposing side as well. Included in this behavior is feigned exposure. Whether the slip is intended or otherwise the auditor or viewer must be careful in interpreting the information given.

EXAMPLE   *Extensive preparation did not prepare the team members in the matter of warranty terms. Member Barnes assumed that their company could offer the standard warranty of three years but Member Young had assumed that warranty, if the issue arose, would be a negotiable item. In response to a remark by the opposing side that it expected a full four year warranty, Barnes blurted out that their standard was three years. At this point Young would have a difficult time using the warranty term as any kind of bargaining chip.*

Soft Bargaining

While there is no official meaning to the term soft bargaining, speakers and writers who use this term mean to distinguish the overtures, and perhaps attitudes, used from those that are more confrontational, more adversarial. Accordingly, seemingly mild behavior irrespective of the intent of the speaker might qualify under this grouping. President Lyndon Johnson's "come let us reason together" and "I will be an honest broker," contain the flavor of soft bargaining from a negotiator who was well known to practice hard hardball. But soft bargaining is more likely identified as an approach where parties attempt to identify the essential worries of both, search for alternatives, while recognizing the ramifications to each side and then forge an agreement to the alternatives that are most mutually satisfying. That is the theory. In practice it is difficult to execute in many types of contracts. Further, some parties declare they practice soft bargaining when they only carry on with a smooth and personal touch in the proceeding.

EXAMPLE *Two negotiating agents pledge to practice the soft bar-*
gaining, I win, you win, or problem solving approach
to reaching agreement. Because in its purest form the
exercise demands "trust," each party must practice rev-
elation. This means that if A has labor problems or B
has financial problems, either of which can affect the
performance of the intended contract, such must be
revealed. What company authorizes such candor, such
trespass of privacy? Further if the contract price could
range between $10,000 and $15,000 (see "utility sched-
ule") what figure is settled on? A explains that it needs
more money because of labor problems, and B likewise
pleads for a very low price because of financial diffi-
culty. As the saying goes, the road to hell is paved with
good intentions. Only "hard bargaining" practices will
resolve these differences and forge an agreement if,
indeed, one can be reached.

Speech Patterns

It is surprising to the interested observer of negotiation sessions
how little attention some participants pay to their own speech
patterns. A review of one's presentation habits includes consideration of both the words used and the tone in which they are
delivered. For those who unintentionally offend by their tone or
language, a friendly critic is recommended. There are, however,
some techniques that are obvious.

EXAMPLE *An agent's presentation was received by the other with*
some resentment which the other tried to conceal. Yet, the
agent's statements about certain qualities expected in the
bargain were, upon reflection, not really too far off base.
The other party became aware of the source of his discon-
tent when he remembered Nietzsche's observation that a
party often contradicts an opinion when what is uncon-
genial is really the tone in which it was conveyed.

Split The Difference

Of all the games bargainers play, the split the difference gambit should always be anticipated. As aspiration points narrow between the parties, continuous mental calculations must be entertained should this old drill be unleashed. Remember, just because this gambit is "old as the hills," a cliché, such platitudes frequently reflect simple truths repeated until people get tired hearing of it. And the truth is that as differences narrow an unspoken (to that point) goal is being approached. Writers remind the bargainers of two things about this announcement. First, the speaker has, without any concession by the other just then made a capitulation of one half of the difference. Secondly, one's concession behavior should always take into account the possible arrival of this statement.

EXAMPLE   *The sticking point in the pending construction contract was the final completion date. The prime contractor had an initial utility schedule (which see) of no earlier than 6 months but aspired for 9 months. The landowner aspired for 4 months completion but would strongly resist anything over 7 months. As the session continued the prime had reduced from 9, to 8.5 to 8 months. The landowner had moved from 3 months, to 3.5 months to 4 months. Observe their positions now, pending a possible "split the difference" offer. If the prime makes the announcement he is momentarily committed to his least desirable option, six months. Even if refused by the landowner the prime has shown willingness to give two months. So too with the landowner using this ploy, showing concession behavior of two months. If both parties are experienced and skillful negotiators neither will make a split-the-difference offer. Given prime's downward resistance point (which see) of 6 months and landowner's upward resistance point of 7 months, agreement is definitely possible and will likely be reached by further offers and counteroffers.*

Standard Form Or Clause

Generally, a negotiator's statement that so and so is a "standard form" or that a particular provision being pressed is a "standard clause" in like situations must be considered to be a tactic. It is a generalization that fills space in the discussion and is delivered, consciously or not, with the intention to intimidate. Apartment managers, for instance, press this point and yet if one examined all the written leases in the building a perfect match might not be found. This is so because in the United States the "freedom of contract" doctrine prevails should the unintimidated choose to exercise this freedom. Expert contractors do prepare form contracts, but the only "standard" is theirs.

EXAMPLE   *Able Systems needs to rent space and because substantial modifications must be made in the premises it demands a long term lease. The landlord resists to some extent but after some battle gives in. A form lease agreement is offered the tenant. Able notices Clause X. In rather mild language it provides that if the landlord sells the building the tenant has six months to vacate the premises. Able objects, the landlords laughs in a somewhat condescending manner, saying, "You must be new to the area, Clause X is a standard term here." Even if that were true, the term cannot be accepted as the long term lease proposal is in reality a six month lease. Clause X (or Ten) in some areas of the country has been in vogue at times.*

Stereotypes

Like the word discrimination, the term stereotype suffers a bad reputation because of the company it keeps. To discriminate (i.e., "to recognize differences") is a proper intellectual exercise but to improperly discriminate (e.g., using differences to determine non-job related hiring) is considered wrong and at times illegal. Nevertheless, the modifier "improperly" is frequently implied by speakers and the present dictionaries confirm as the secondary meaning is listed as "to act on the basis of prejudice." Yet stereotyping is merely generalization, a practice hardly without its uses. Behaviorists study how people act and they describe patterns that the scientists consider likely to be repeated by many individuals within that group. Negotiation practices are, of course, behavioral activity at its most subtle and critical. Once

warned of the possibility, the careful negotiator is prepared to determine whether 1) such a pattern might occur in the sessions and 2) how the particulars of one's own behavior might be modified to restrict the mischief. The more obvious applications of the term are found where parties of different cultures.

EXAMPLE   *Accurate or not, the American style of negotiations, the hard bargaining and the poker game, combined with impulsive thrusts, needs to be restrained in some environments, at least until the measure of the opponent is determined. While negotiators in the USA, like those in Germany and Russia, have an apparently high tolerance for confrontation, the South Koreans, for instance, normally do not, and it is traditionally considered "bad show" to the English, whose penchant for civility is crested with good humor and a sociable manner. The applicability of these apparent stereotypes must be tested until the enquiring and observant negotiator finds that they are irrelevant to the parties who are now before them. It has been observed that not all Chinese are concerned about losing face.*

Straddling A Chair

Research might reveal why this particular behavior pattern in the United States is generally interpreted to show assurance (command or arrogance) in the actor. However, as long as many bargainers sense that this is an aggressive act it demands that they pay attention. The obvious question is why does a straddler entertain such assurance? Here the psyche of the other is tested. Does such behavior intimidate or, to the comfortable party merely reflect questionable manners of the actor?

EXAMPLE   *Aster is considered a crackerjack sales person. Everyone is his friend, or so it seems. His habit of straddling a chair during a negotiating session is interesting. Is the practice*

just poor manners, or does he indeed feel that it is not necessary for him to sit as everyone else does? If it is the latter, and not just boorish behavior, the other party might speculate as to why Aster does something that seems to show he holds others in low esteem.

Substitute Performance

One of the more interesting negotiation moves occurs in the post-contracting phase. Most business persons recognize that absolute compliance with contractual terms becomes increasingly difficult as the performance promised is intricate (i.e. by reason of technical or drafting defects) or contains many different undertakings. Much bargaining occurs in this post-contractual period. At law the term substitute performance generally refers to responsibilities where delivery or payment problems arise. However, in negotiation parlance one might press for substitute performance where a party can't exactly perform for business reasons. This type of conflict does not differ from the types of bargaining used in forming the underlying contract which is now under review.

EXAMPLE   *The contract called for the manufacture and delivery of special technical machinery with tolerances that the performer discovered it could not meet. This is a common occurrence where at negotiation time the parties failed to appreciate that either the anticipated method is not financially or technically feasible, or the performer has insufficient expertise or equipment to perform. It is at this point that litigation arises because of one or several of the causes listed. Here the parties may "go back to the drawing board," amend the contract, and try again. Case litigation reflects that expertise in drafting the new agreement is essential.*

Sweetener

One person's sweetener can qualify as another's trade off item (which see). The problem with sweeteners is that they occasionally masquerade as something unethical if not illegal. Where the item or service is offered to move the other party toward a deal two questions must be asked. One, is the item or service being offered to the party in interest, and two, is such offering a natural component of the deal? If both questions cannot be answered in the affirmative, the sweetener may fail to meet a legal or ethical test.

EXAMPLE   *Barrow is a follower of the cultural habit attributed to some countries, that is, that one must "grease" the wheels to move the wagon. "Gift giving" is his forte and such are sent to employees of prospective clients as a matter of course. Such conduct is questioned on both tests, one, the gift is to one not entitled to it, and two it is not relevant to the transaction. A sweetener in a negotiation would be a concession offered during the bargaining period where, for instance, a promised warranty for two years is extended to three to move the deal toward fulfillment. Such an action clearly meets both legal and ethical tests.*

Tactics

This term was apparently borrowed from the military. Where strategy deals with overall objectives and multiple moves, a behavior that qualifies as a tactic has a specific target. There is no French Academy of Letters informing the unlearned as to the names of various tactics and the behaviors they identify. Low-balling, for example, has a number of different behavior scenarios (which see). So too with the "Missing Element Maneuver," as it could involve a party, a document, or some other element. The purpose of a particular behavior pattern is to move a certain agenda that the user has in mind.

EXAMPLE   *When the negotiator host sets the guest chairs in a particular location (venue games, which see), or one party asks for your help with the price (transference, bogey, which see) the object of the aggressor is to make a particular point. These are tactics. Not all tactics are unfairly manipulative, but their deployment sometimes justifies the victim to conclude that the other party can't see a belt without hitting below it.*

Take It or Leave It

Does there breathe a party, who, fed up with the behavior of another, and wishing to deliver a climactic force to the proceedings has not been tempted to shout, "Take it or leave it!" The controlled negotiator is only tempted; but the rest of us occasionally surrender to the natural impulse to take it. While some writers explain how this ultimatum can be used as a tactic, it must be practiced carefully. Further, because this hackneyed mantra is likely to have an element of confrontation, the prospective target must be one that will not react emotionally (e.g. cut off his nose to spite his face) by "leaving."

EXAMPLE   *One bargainer is exasperated. The other is truly being unreasonable. Shock treatment may have to be employed. Yet how to do it without killing the potential deal? Some do it lightly, and rapidly, such as the soft, "Gosh, it looks like it's the best I can do!" This follows the old caveat that instructs that in skating over thin ice safety lies in speed.*

Team Playing

Certain bargaining sessions require more than one player per side. They are usually called teams. It may be that some members have different functions. One could be the technical expert and the other the generalist. In such an instance there is frequently a natural division of duties which each honors.

However, team members must be instructed with particular care; their roles, and sometimes their presentations, must be carefully controlled and even rehearsed. One distinctive team playing scenario is in stereotypical "good cop, bad cop." (which see) practice.

EXAMPLE   *The difficulty with having more than one party negotiate is the possibility that the other side may have been given raised expectations. It is not unusual, in the oil business, for example, for the buyer's engineer or technician to have had contact with the supplier. It could be a lunch situation where the technician has informed the supplier of its need of a certain type of equipment and of the technician's belief that only the supplier's product will do. The failure of the buyer to appreciate that this encounter with the technical people constitutes a team effort, with all its concomitant risks and advantages, could be costly. Telling your people not to talk informally with the other side sounds like easy advice to give, but it is amazing how often it is simply ignored.*

Telephone Negotiations

While bargaining over the telephone has a number of drawbacks, the practice is a reality that firms must live with. Advice in this area concentrates on defense. It is taught that since the caller has the advantage the callers's preparation must be countered by the callee. The prudent caller would have a basic script or "story line" crafted before calling, including, if appropriate, necessary data to use to persuade or respond to potential arguments. The absence of physical presence leaves both sides weak in interpreting body signals; accordingly the exact words used by the other should be noted. Many telephone negotiations fall in the quick negotiation category in which there tends to be a big loser and big winner.

EXAMPLE   *Gardall was surprised to receive a telephone call from a prospective buyer who had been written off several weeks ago when the meetings had proved fruitless. "We have a need that must be met on a rush basis," began the buyer's agent. "Here is what we need from you: one, an immediate answer, yes or no, $740 is the price, which as you must realize is close to your last figure, the 40 units we talked about, 10% penalty termination clause and delivery within 30 days. What do you say?" Gardall must be prepared to exercise a few defense moves that unobtrusively activate delay on the issue until he can carefully evaluate the "offer." Perhaps something like this: "Sounds promising, let me get my file and call you right back or let me check with production so that we can put this together, etc." The risk of making a poor deal*

with an immediate response is probably greater than the risk of losing the order by not responding immediately.

Throwaways

To the expert negotiator there are no "throwaways." To the knowledgeable negotiator a throwaway is a disguised trade off (which see) item. Throwaways are usually inexpensive items, but the skilled negotiator will craft those that have some appeal to the other party.

EXAMPLE   *Mikler has developed the use of throwaways to something like an art. He takes careful note of what throwaway items appear to have been most appreciated by those with whom he negotiates. For example, he has found that just a bit lower interest rate (6.3% v. 6.4%) has great appeal even if its actual value in financing purchased equipment is only a few dollars. Another throwaway valued by many parties is even a minor increase in the length of a warranty, such as 25 months instead of 24.*

Time Investment Theory

All of us have a limited time on earth, and many (perhaps most) people don't want to admit that some of their time has been wasted. They want results in exchange for the time they have invested in negotiation, whether personal or business. To the negotiator, the application of the time investment theory becomes a valuable tool in dealing with some bargainers. Simply, some parties press on, to their disadvantage and discomfort, despite the fact that the attainment of an appealing ending is unlikely.

EXAMPLE   *The stereotypical car dealer experience benefits from the behavior of those who just don't know when to walk away*

TIME INVESTMENT THEORY

and accept that their time has been wasted. Most car buyers have at one time or another faced a salesperson who spends considerable time with them, going over various matters, including the personal life of the buyer. Finally the salesperson writes up the "contract." (i.e., really just a piece of paper) has the buyers sign it (the salesperson does not) and then "takes it to the Manager for an okay." Not likely. The buyers stew for some "time." Finally, the salesperson returns with some changes on the "contract," all in favor of the dealer. That is the "best that the Manager can do." So more haggling continues. Enough prospective buyers, although insulted and miffed at this behavior, do not leave.

Instead they press on, having invested this much unpleasant time, their gut feel is that they cannot write off the time they have invested in trying to make a deal. Some research has indicated that for many buying a car is more unpleasant than visiting a dentist for a root canal. Many car buyers are the victims of the time investment theory and settle with the salesperson on less attractive terms.

Timing

Negotiation literature abounds with stories regarding timing, including such practices as setting agendas, discovering the opponent's airline departure time, imminent withdrawal of offers, availability schedules and the like. Experienced practitioners practice restraint when timing maneuvers are being used against them. One of the difficulties attorneys have with business clients (or witnesses for their clients) in depositions or courtroom appearances is getting them to listen to a question in its entirety and taking their time to formulate their answer before giving it.

EXAMPLE   *Negotiators recognize weakness in others in the way they ignore the importance of timing. Students can sometimes be trained by an appreciation of the following exercise. The lecturer instructs one student to ask two questions of him. The first is: "What is one of your greatest pleasures? This question is to be followed by "And what is your greatest difficulty in doing so?" The student obeys and the lecturer responds that "telling traveling salesmen jokes is one of my greatest pleasures." The student then asks the second question. As the student reaches the word "greatest" the lecturer interrupts and blurts out "timing." How often in the heat of "haggling" does one choose the wrong moment to bring up a point or interrupt the other and incorrectly predict the full question?*

Trade Off Preparation

A certain percentage of negotiations require careful investigation and planning prior to beginning the bargaining (i.e., dickering) stage. Accordingly, a prudent manager will determine what terms are essential, what the company could live with and what it absolutely could not tolerate. In any extended negotiation, there appear moments when each side would like to give concessions **but needs a reason to do so**. Sometimes, for example, an offer of a trade-off item allows the other side to back down from a tough position or from a deadlock. This practice allows for "face saving."

EXAMPLE   *Your company provides a standard warranty on certain sales. However this is not a given because circumstances might dictate that the standard warranty is inappropriate for a potential customer. Should you be required to offer a warranty it would be important that such a concession, or the quality of it (e.g. one year, two years), is saved to trade for some feature or concession from the other.*

Trade Offs

The practice of using your assets to buy other assets. In most negotiations there are certain promises or commitments that have value to the other side. Experienced bargainers have carefully assembled these (see trade off preparation, above), and come to the session armed to use them to gain benefits from the other side. Social scientists, and one's's own experience, tells negotiators that it is a common error to assume that terms, seemingly valueless to you, have no value to others.

EXAMPLE   *In purchasing copper tubing your evaluation of the needs of the company is as follows:*
  1. *A low price is essential.(-1)*
  2. *Minor variations in quality are not critical. (0)*

  3. *A price revision under an escalator clause would be permitted (+1)*
  4. *A termination clause must be favorable (-1)*
  5. *Certainty of delivery dates would be helpful (0)*

  Observe the weights (+, -, or 0), or company values, assigned by this manager in the planning stage to these potential terms in a contract. This is almost always done, whether consciously or not. During the heat of the dickering stage the weights may be forgotten. By recognizing this exercise consciously and its conclusions, however, the bargainer is more likely to employ these judgments in a timely and effective manner. Treat the quality variations, price revisions and delivery dates as possible "trade-offs" which may be used during negotiations. Surrender them only for a real trade. The "minus" items are considered to be non-negotiable unless modified by major and unexpected concessions by the other side.

Transference

"My budget allows only X dollars, and your price list is nearly double, can you help me?" This revelation and plea attempts to shift one's problem or weakness on the other. However, revealing weaknesses has its own risks. It can allow an experienced negotiator an opportunity to now reshape the announced need of the other, leaving the other bound with an admitted position (e. g. "Budget allows only X dollars") This practice of transference, sometimes called the "Bogey" (Chester Karrass) or "Monkey on the Back" raises an interesting psychological premise. On one hand it is patently flattering to be asked to help, but there is a competing view which may be taken by the other. Some individuals consider pleas for help from otherwise competent individuals to run counter to the maxim that "one does not convert one's own needs into the other party's duties."

EXAMPLE   *The scene is a convention for purchasing agents. One of the speakers represents a major supplier of material. She has titled her speech, "Let Us Help Produce Quality." The speaker explains how the firm's experts are in place to help with any purchasing problem. "Place your difficulties in our hands." This qualifies as an offer by the speaker to have the "monkey" put on her firm's back. She is asking for transference to be practiced by prospective customers. It is likely that this supplier has thought this out and that their willingness to take on their customers' problems have calculated benefits to the firm.*

Type A (Conflict) Problem

Most commercial negotiations fall in this category because of the circumstances preceding the encounter between the parties. After all, it is only rational that most meetings occur because the parties have already determined that each has the potential to satisfy the other. Rarely are they in error in this judgment that the conflict is a Type A one.

EXAMPLE   *Gordon Fabricating's research has uncovered that the specialized material needed is supplied by Firms A, B and C in the region. Because Gordon is in the position to buy, and the firms hold themselves out as sellers, the reasonable conclusion is that any negotiation conflict will be resolved in the main, with details as to price, quantity, delivery, quality and credit being malleable issues subject to solutions.*

Type A "Stuff"

Apparently, borrowing from psychology research, many consider the term Type A to identify conduct practiced by parties who seem driven. They tend to speak rapidly and aggressively, frequently interrupting the speaker. As a negotiator it is useful to be aware of this generalization but such appreciation is needed if only to assist in evaluating the conduct as natural to the party or whether it is a feigned approach. In negotiation, a stressful time, such personality differences are not always evident. Some psychological research offers that anticipated threats from opponents tend to minimize the manifestation of personality extremes. Simply, a Type A person aware of possible negative consequences from such conduct may practice restraint.

EXAMPLE   *Back at the office Mary is excitable and quick to jump at conclusions. She is, however, a crackerjack negotiator on the road. Somehow, she reacts to the risky task of dealing with the other party for real money and real company interests by subduing her general Type A behavior pattern. She would add to the literature that suggests that threat tends to reduce all of us to a common denominator. Lawyers witness this change in behavior in opponents in the courtroom as judges reduce polemics to reality.*

Type B Behavior

Correctly or not, conduct that is seemingly non-confrontational is frequently identified as type B behavior. However, there is no guarantee that such behavior will result in agreement being reached. The negotiating session may be a pleasant experience up to a point where, sooner or later, the parties will have to get down to business.

EXAMPLE *The response, "Come, let us look at this issue from your side and see whether we have something to offer you," after being attacked by the other is considered to be conduct that those that practice civility prize.*

Type B Conflict

Behavioralists study conflict among parties from a number of angles. When concluding that the differences between parties are (strangely) unrecognized, the analyst identifies that this is a type B conflict. The assessment is that any agreement will be reached only with great difficulty. Falling in this group are those frequently nebulous situations where one asks oneself just what is the real issue here and why are we having this trouble? Some have characterized Type B conflict as "dancing around the May pole." That is, there is no real movement toward agreement despite many pleasantries and great civility.

EXAMPLE   *Otto, an experienced negotiator, was puzzled at the seeming lack of response by the other party's team. They were polite, but would not make concrete counter proposals, merely indicating dissatisfaction with each of the several offers that Otto's team had made. Otto became increasingly frustrated and finally said, "Look, what's going on here? All you say is you aren't happy with any of our proposals but you won't make any of your own. Why did you even bother to schedule this meeting?" At this point the meeting broke up, amicably, and Otto's team left. Only later did Otto find out that it was unlikely that the two companies would ever get togther. His firm wanted a low price above all, and would therefore expect a low standard of quality. The other firm was very jealous of its reputation, would only produce at an expensive high quality level and consequently required a high price for its product.*

Umbrella Issues

To some it's an open question as to whether knowledge of your opponent's overall concerns and ambitions in a pending bargaining session greatly assists a person in being an effective negotiator. While the axiom "knowledge is power" carries weight in general, awareness of the other's primary concern is not necessarily helpful. This possibility exists because only the disciplined handle advantages well. An umbrella issue, as used both in negotiation and in general comment, refers to an overriding concern of the negotiator's company. It can be as simple as garnering new contracts with little concern as to their quality, or the development of an image in the industry, or the wish to beat out an annoying competitor even at considerable cost.

EXAMPLE   *An attorney was instructed by an insurance company to obtain cancellation of a ten-year insurance policy held by a lessee of an airport concession. The attorney, in studying the file, noted that the insurer's monetary risk was minimal because of the language of the airport lease. The premiums, however, were substantial. The attorney advised the insurer that he did not recommend the proposed cancellation, citing his legal analysis. The insurer curtly ordered the attorney to do as he was told. The attorney negotiated as instructed at some cost to the insurer. Only later did the attorney learn that the insurer was applying for a better national insurance rating. The presence of a ten-year-term policy of this type made this company ineligible to qualify for a sought-for insurance industry rating. The "umbrella issue," unspoken and unrevealed, was the rating game, not benefits flowing from an obviously lucrative premium.*

Uniform Commercial Code

This body of statutory law governs many of the legal rules of contracts among negotiators. These principles are, at some critical times, strikingly different than the general law of contracting. This is particularly true in the silent (called "implied") terms the law places on business transactions. Simply, where parties are silent, even important terms are assumed by the law to be such and such. While many negotiators have had formal business training where some law has been part of their study, it is necessary that certain special rules regarding contract formation techniques in regard to sales of goods, quality commitments (i.e, warranty doctrines) and performance obligations be studied.

EXAMPLE   *Brad is new to negotiating. He didn't realize that many oral commitments regarding sales of goods can be legally binding, despite the dollar amount. He learned this the hard way when a confirmatory memo reached his desk. Further, Brad thought himself quite safe in making no explicit quality commitments to a buyer. He did not realize that his silence created a powerful warranty of merchantability in the hands of the buyer. Further, he has been told that he has just been burned by the doctrine of "battle of the forms." This refers to the practice of contracting by sending the company's proposed contract printed form as an initial move or as a reply. By now, Brad is not a happy camper; he realizes that before he does any more contract negotiating he is going to have to study the provisions of the Uniform Commercial Code in detail.*

Utility Schedule

The awareness of the meaning of utility schedules alerts the bargainer to the dynamics of the give and take in a session. It tells one that what he or she offers can alter the behavior of the other in an instant. The theory underlying utility schedules is based on the reality of the rapid movement of positions in a bargaining session. Normally, the positions involve each party's resistance point and aspiration level. Each thrust by one party can affect the other.

EXAMPLE   *You have secretly learned a seller will resist at a price lower than $10 per unit but has aspirations for $15. This may be called the seller's "utility schedule." When the time comes to make a first bid what should you start with: $8, $10 or $14? The academics tell us that your selection will alter the seller's utility schedule. A first bid of $14, for example, likely changes the seller's aspirations, who now raises it several dollars. Contrariwise, a bid of $8 would incline the seller to rethink that $15 aspiration.*

Venue Games

In the real estate business the mantra is "location, location, location." Some negotiators adopt this cry when they manipulate the physical aspects of the meeting place. These features might appear as a particular city, building, or room. The room has its uses as the place for fashioning such items as the.type of furniture, the lighting, and even the placement and elevation of tables and chairs. Further, personnel may play a role as they make planned entrances and exits during the session. Like many theories, there are both advantages and disadvantages to using the venue in this calculated way.

EXAMPLE   *Margo was a believer in settings. She had exquisite taste and understood how to express both class and authority. She was not above arranging chairs and tables in such a way as to place another in the position*

of being entertained yet impressed and, to a degree, intimidated. The degree to which the particular "other" is influenced by the setting determines the success of the tactic. Experienced bargainers would not be influenced by this display. Nor, in other contexts, would they put up with poor or misdirected lighting, uncomfortable chairs, ringing telephones (cell or regular) in the room, etc.

Weak Position

One part of the preparation stage includes a review of the firm's weaknesses in the upcoming negotiation and steps to be taken

to counter the opponent's use of them during the bargaining. Experience teaches that not all fears are realized. In the first place, one party's shortcoming may never be known by the other and, more important, there is the probability that the opponent has its own concerns about its position. Further, not all weaknesses are relevant to the other party except perhaps for use as negotiation thrusts.

EXAMPLE   *Runnymeade has been suffering sporadic production delays due to work stoppages in one department. Attempting to deal with Tailorette, the agents for Runnymeade prepared an elaborate plan by which delivery delays would be compensated under a liquidated damage clause should Tailorette learn of Runnymeade's troubles and demand assurances. On the other side of the table Tailorette had its own troubles, mainly cash flow, and concentrated on how they could handle the payment terms. Here, each side has a significant bargaining weakness. The question is: who will blink first?*

What If

Among the methods employed to restart a stalled engine are those practices which give the listener an opportunity to look at the situation in a more attractive way. But first, the other side must be soothed if a sensitive nerve has been touched. The phrase "what if" followed by a statement offering some hope to the other is one such method. At its least the practice is verbal balm which attempts to restore the session to a more amiable atmosphere. At its best it offers the other an opportunity to save face and consider other terms where unpleasant propositions may have dealt the negotiation certain damage.

EXAMPLE   *It became apparent that the detailed inspection package demanded by the buyer had ruffled the seller, who had reacted to the proposal as an insult to the seller's reputation for quality. Sensing the touchiness of the situation, but unwilling to completely abandon its felt need for quality protection at delivery, the buyer's negotiator attempted to ease the situation by saying, "What if some of your people could work with ours when we take delivery which would speed up the process and have our quality control people get to know yours better?"*

Yessable Questions

There are some people who are negative in their approach to life; they may have been born to this condition. But someone

who wishes to persuade others must not be one of.those. "Getting to yes" is a talent practiced by the deliberate negotiator. While it takes more than personality, there is some truth in the saying that charm is a way of garnering an affirmative response without having asked a clear question. The practice of asking questions which suggest positive responses is an acquired talent. A very useful approach involves the formation of solutions in a multiple choice form. Another is the crafting of questions which are structured to encourage a positive response.

EXAMPLE   *There is an old salesperson's technique that makes this point. Simply, the practical peddler would asks the customer, "Do you want the blue or the gray suit, or both?" The unasked question (does one want to buy any?) is discreetly masked. Like many platitudes, old advice seldom gets the credit it deserves. Frequently, a platitude is simply a truth repeated until others get tired of hearing it. Skillful bargainers craft yessable questions.*

Zero Defects

In the popular sense zero defects refers to a concept used in "quality" programs, commonly associated with the manufacturing process. This phrase is sometimes tossed about carelessly during negotiation banter. Historically it has been difficult to achieve zero defects in a manufacturing process. However, in recent years the concepts of W. Edwards Deming, as applied by the Japanese using *kanban* and just-in-time techniques enabled many manufacturing processes to produce zero, or near zero, defective products. For the purchaser to whom quality is important, the inquiry is whether a supplier's claimed zero defects program is truly effective, somewhat effective, or is it just smoke?

EXAMPLE   *The widgets produced by Widget Mase are of excellent quality, well above the tolerances standard in the industry.*

The product is not perfect however. In their attempt to continue to improve, the firm appoints a team, a committee to manage the Zero Defect (ZD) program. The directive to all parties in the chain is to do things right the first time. It may be many months before the initial program ends, at which time new standards or goals are set. When Barrow hears the words "zero defects" used by an agent of Widget Mase, a prospective supplier, she might delve into the meaning of that phrase at Widget Mase. It could be that the firm has a ZD "program" that is poorly constructed, poorly executed, or both.

PART THREE

The Tests

Are You A "Born" Negotiator?

What is your underlying negotiation temperament, your basic inclination so to speak?

Take this little test. Only you will know the suggested analysis so you may be frank about your behavior.

1. A respected real estate agent has in good faith spent considerable time and effort in an effort to encourage you to sign. You find the proposition solid and intend to sign the contract the next day. You now have changed your mind.

    How uncomfortable will you be with yourself as you break the bad news to the agent?
    A. Very
    B. Slightly
    C. Moderately so.

2. You are to make a contract presentation having a number of tough items to a party you do not know very well.

    You are more likely to assume that this party
    A. Has less advantages, or edges, than you at the meeting.
    B. Has more of such.
    C. You assume that both of you are about even in that department.

3. You have come across inside (secret) information about the seller with whom you are about to negotiate. You have learned that this seller aspires to get $10 a unit for her product but has authority to drop as low as $7 per unit.

It is time for you to name a figure. Your first offer is which of the following?

A. $9
B. $6
C. $8

See Answers page 198

Do You Agree With These Generalizations?

Some negotiation behavioral traits, innate or formed, seem to help; others don't fare so well. Take this little test and see how your views conform to those of negotiation experts.

1. Able has always been confident, during college and beyond. Moreover, the "glass was always half full," or would be by the time she got through. High aspiration was her motto but it difficult to understand why she continued with such a mental stand for she was not that successful in getting what she wanted. She is being trained to negotiate. Which of the following statements do you think she is being taught?
   A. Persons with high aspirations "win" most benefits in negotiations.
   B. The confidence that one can persuade others, called Machivellism, is the key to successful negotiations.
   C. Parties with great expectations have a strong edge in negotiations over parties having more modest goals.

2. Baker is an aggressive type. He comes prepared but lacks a smooth delivery which would assist his inner drive to succeed. Baker is told one of these statements is false. Which conclusion is considered by researchers as *false*?
   A. One should never make large initial demands.
   B. The party making the largest single concession is likely to end up with a poor deal.

C. Success in negotiation is not generally inhibited by making a high and surprising initial offer.

3. Charlene thinks she can read people quite well. This is particularly true of opponents in bargaining sessions. Obstinate at times, she also thinks she is a whiz on the telephone as her quick mind seems to catch the other side off guard. Charlene would not be happy changing her style. She was displeased to learn that researchers do not agree with everything she believes. Which one statement below is considered to be an *incorrect* generalization about negotiations and negotiators?
    A. An experienced bargainer is better at reading the wants and needs of the opposition than is a novice negotiator.
    B. Abrupt negotiations, such as telephone transactions, are more likely to end in extreme results.
    C. Hardheaded bargainers deadlock more frequently than do more agreeable parties, but do not necessarily do poorly in most completed sessions.

4. Dixon is an overachiever because he assumed that he had fewer talents than others. Further, he is always a little unhappy after a session, believing that if he had a better education, a more distinguished speaking voice, and a clearer complexion things would have been different. Dixon might be interested in the following conclusions. Which statement is considered *incorrect*?
    A. Negotiators tend to think that the other parties have more clout than they actually do have.
    B. At the end of a negotiation few parties believe that they have done poorly.
    C. Many negotiators do not even know that they are practicing a tactic.

See Answers page 200

How Well Do You Dance?
The Utility Schedule

The term "utility schedule" is used in different disciplines and contexts. In negotiation parlance it refers to the *status quo* point (i.e., when parties fail to agree). Each schedule then has two components: a party's "resistance point" and this party's "level of aspiration." Simply, it is illustrated by a buyer who has been instructed to pay no more than $10,000 (resistance point), but to try to come back with a signed contract for $7,500 (aspiration level).

This simple formula however must be commented on when viewing the dynamics of a negotiation. In order to show how fragile and fading this schedule is assume the following set of facts:

Assume that you have secretly discovered your seller's *resistance point* and her *level of aspiration*. She does not know yours, however. Specifically, you have learned that she is prepared to lower the price for the goods for no less than $12,500 (i.e., *resistance point*). Further, her hope (i.e. *aspiration level*) is to get you to buy for $17,000.

After some discussion the seller makes her first offer. It is $20,500. You haggle and she insists, and it is appropriate for you to make a counteroffer.

Which of the following bids would you make?
1. $9,000
2. $11,000
3. $11,500

4. $12,500
5. $13,800

Before you look at the suggested answer, examine the reason why you selected the particular number.

See Answers page 202

How Well Do You Practice Concessions?
The Monetary Increment Game

Counteroffers in the bidding (or bickering) stage are the dance steps; lead with a discordant step and the dance, for the perpetrator at least, can be costly. Simply, sometimes a wrong step (bid) can occur in the heat of the discussion because the dancers are not paying attention and they are not too sharp at simple arithmetic, specifically percentages. Here is a little test to remind you of one way in which you can send a message to the other side that advances your interest.

For those who play bridge or know about the card game the signal calling seems familiar. The uninformed might question, rightly, "Why use an opening bid of two no trump? Come right out and say you have 22 to 24 points with stoppers and balanced distribution. The answer: that is not permitted; bridge has rules: parties may use approved signals but may not pass on explicit information. So too with negotiation. A party, for example, may want to lead the opposite party to a particular dollar amount or other quantitative term (e.g. 60 day delivery rather than 20 day delivery) but one can't just come out and say such a thing.

Let's see how this can be exampled.

Assume that a negotiator has been instructed to purchase an incinerator system (e.g. fancy name for furnace) for an executive office building. The prospective buyer possesses many of the relevant details such as the dimensions of the cavity, the needs of the building (e.g., handles both wet and dry garbage), and the different models available from the vendor. Model X-400, the engineers tell the buyer, would be a good fit. The list price in the vendor's catalog is $47,500. After the preliminaries are past (e.g, weather, "great game last night," respective comments about each other's firms, the first rate quality of the systems, etc.) the vendor comes out strong saying that their list price is being raised next month to $51,200 due to demand and increased manufacturing cost. However, since the catalog has been seen by the prospective buyer they will honor the catalogue figure. Now the haggling begins. Besides the figures set below there is a great deal of dialogue (see carrying words, generalization, etc.). While all this is going on any one of these three sequences of bids could be made by the buyer as the seller makes counteroffers each time.

Bidder A	begins with 39,000	then 43,500	then 44,000
Bidder B	begins with 39,000	then 42,000	then 44,000.
Bidder C	begins with 39,000	then 41,500	then 44,000

Remember the message. The buyer intends to lead the other to the proper territory. Generally, misdirection in this aspect of the negotiation is unproductive. Which one of the bidding sequences is trying to influence the other into anticipating the final figure? Simply, which of these bids reflects acting purposely and with sincerity?

See Answers page 204

Can You Spot A Tactic?

Some "show business" in negotiations has been labeled as tactics. The term "tactics" has been defined as the technique or science of securing objectives set by strategy. However, in bargaining, this conduct is no more than common behavior patterns long practiced by actors both consciously and unconsciously. There is no official name given to a particular pattern of behavior but the labels mentioned below are common.

1. Jasmine has been an agent for Tanner Entities for 20 years. The company has been bought out and restructuring is beginning to take place. In the meantime Jasmine is out doing her job. In her latest assignment with an old customer she pleads, "Tom, help me out here with some good terms. My job is under review and with Mom in the hospital you know how stressful this time is for me." Jasmine is using:

   A   The transference tactic.
   B   The personalization tactic.
   C   The impossible offer tactic.

2. Laura has had two meetings with this firm. It seems that a closing is imminent but there is always some one thing that yet needs to be done by the other side. Laura can't understand why they don't anticipate this and be prepared for the closing. Is the firm so poorly organized, or is this just a way of testing her patience? Laura should consider that a particular tactic may be in play here. Which one is it possibly?

    A. The missing element tactic.
    B. They are cherry picking.
    C. They are seeking "freebies."

3. Thompson can't believe his ears. This supplier right out of the box is willing to stay within Thompson's first figures and the promised performance is an almost unbelievably short delivery time, a commitment that seemed impossible when dealing with other suppliers. What should Thompson consider when viewing this possible good fortune?
    A. The other firm is in financial trouble.
    B. He has finally found a fine and reputable contractor.
    C. He has just met a lowballer.

4. Heather is tuned a bit high; she is a Type A personality. Her firm, however, likes this nervousness, this show of a high level of energy and concern over little things as well as big issues. An offer that she had been waiting for has been faxed in from a firm and while the terms are not quite to her liking they could be accepted. The last line in the message however, disturbed her. It made her nervous. It stated "due to circumstances beyond our control this offer is only good until today's closing time at our office in Los Angeles, 5:00 PST, 8:00 P.M. your time in New York." Heather wonders what that is all about. One real possibility is that:
    A. She is dealing with a highly efficient company.
    B. She is being treated to the "deadline technique."
    C. This firm is dominated by aggressive contractors.

5. Taylor admits that his boss is one smooth operator, having been a crackerjack negotiator for over twenty years before being shipped upstairs. She does know the industry well as well as the type of issues that arise in typical transactions. Taylor has one complaint, however, his boss

has never explained why he must frequently check back with her on some detail of a proposed deal. It gets kind of embarrassing sometimes to put off a commitment when everything looks like a go. But most of the time, he admits, the delay did seem to make a better deal in the end. What conclusion should he draw from his boss's behavior?

- A. She is manifesting her lack of confidence in his ability.
- B. She is arming him with the "limits of authority" ploy.
- C. She is to teach him how to aggravate the other side.

6. Gatter is the perfect actor for this tactic. Gatter is highly competent, in command of the facts of each transaction and is patient. He sets a figure or term which he will not budge from. This figure or term is handsomely below list or the expected price from the other, or the term is a real imposition on the other. He can make his voice whiney and pleading; he is convincing. His favorite pitch is, "Charlie, I know we should not be even approaching you on this, but we figured you were at least entitled to hear us out. We need your Model 65C. I know, I know, it's your finest and lists for $72,500 and I am sure worth every cent of it. However, our budget number is carved in stone. Not a penny over $66,500. Can you help us out here at all?" What is this type of behavior called?

- A. The old "lowballing" technique.
- B. The "transference" technique
- C. The "cherry picking" technique

7. Maddeline is charming. She has a patter worthy of a successful confessor as she dwells on your interests, not her own. But gosh, is she slow. There is always some alley she goes down, comes back and then reviews. She is so patient. The funny part is that it looks like the party has a

deal but some little point comes up that Maddeline can't get approval for. She does want to make a deal but you wish she could be more forthcoming about these little points which seem to crop up during the negotiation. What could Maddeline be relying on to advance her interest?

A. The benefits that flow from using the "cherry picking" technique

B. The benefits that flow from using the "time investment theory" technique.

C. The benefits that flow from the "I win you win" technique.

See Answers page 205

How Sensitive Are You To The Negotiator's Background?

Obviously a bargainer should not unintentionally offend the other party by speech or otherwise. Even in dealing with a person of similar background it still is possible to unconsciously do something that "turns that person off." The risk is increased when negotiating with parties from different backgrounds. The other party's background might be a different nationality, culture, religion, or even a region. While one should not assume that a negotiator from a different background would necessarily behave or react according to some observed traits common to such background, it would be unwise to ignore the possibility in the particular.

An American dealing with a Mexican firm, for example, should not complain about a delay in providing information by even jokingly noting "Yes, I understand, that can be done "mañana." Or, even a pleasant inquiry into the ancestry of a bargainer from Sydney might offend. Latins are not happy with the idea that they have been labeled as putting off matters for another day and certainly Australians have heard and read enough about the social status of many of the early English settlers on that continent. Further, some cultures are not comfortable with the practice of "directly getting down to business;" accordingly a smoother introductory phase would be recommended when dealing with parties from that culture until one is sure it is not applicable to the parties in the present negotiation.

International observers and the literature suggest many of the obvious generalizations listed below. These generalizations could assist in evaluating the trading environment. What is your guess about the following behavior or negotiating characteristics.?

1. In the United States "grease payments" refer to benefits given to a prospective contractor to assist the bargaining process. Under the Foreign Corrupt Practices Act some types of payments are illegal when dealing with international firms. It would be easy to take outward offense when "extras" or "sweeteners" are suggested or demanded. Which of the following would more likely interpret the offer as non offensive?
   A. A negotiator from London
   B. A negotiator from Quito
   C. A negotiator from Bombay

2. Some negotiators tend to practice an organized style of bargaining. This grew from formal training techniques in argument. These parties do not proceed to the bottom line immediately but work with an outline of agreement centering on the establishment of principles. Such bargainers, who prefer using their own language, are more likely to have been trained where?
   A. Rome
   B. Paris
   C. San Francisco

3. Business parties from this region are perceived as confident, easy going and flexible. Accordingly they speak well but not hurriedly and keep their public profile moderate. They expect the others to be adaptable, a trait not generally experienced in many of the cultures. Parties from their region tend to believe that they are well received in most parts of the world. They are likely from:

A. Athens
B. Vienna
C. Stockholm

4. Bargaining with teams is not uncommon. Teams by their nature require a leader. Some team members honor this leadership in the bargaining session by deferring to the team member with the superior position. A team from which of the following would be more likely to bow to rank?
   A. London
   B. New York
   C. Milan

5. These bargainers tend to speak faster than what is generally practiced world-wide. While they attempt to show sincerity they treat the session as a contest which must be begun sooner than later. They are well versed in "tactics" and use them. You might recognize them as being from:
   A. Manila
   B. Chicago
   C. Berlin

6. Historically these business people do not like to believe that they are "in trade." This has lead to the perception that they do not prepare for the upcoming session as thoroughly as parties from a different background. Nevertheless these individuals are sociable and to a certain extent flexible. You might run across them in
   A. Manchester
   B. Bangkok
   C. Stuttgart

7. Accurately or not, these contractors are perceived as usually exuding good cheer and quite interested in developing the social aspects of the relationship. Body language is

quite apparent, and narrowing the business issues between the parties cannot be rushed. Bluntness is not advised in dealing with such individuals. Such parties are likely from such places as

A. Brisbane

B. Bogota

C. Nassau

8. Trust in the promises and representations of the other are important to these negotiators. Accordingly, the details of the bargain play a secondary role while these parties attempt to take the measure of the other. Such an investigation takes time and once these parties are satisfied about the bona fides of the other, the specifics of the deal are much easier and quickly settled on. Where might you experience this behavior?

A. Oslo

B. Marseille

C. Riyadh

9. These participants are perceived as somewhat difficult to negotiate with. Discreet behavior is expected and the position of the other in a firm is important. Haggling is not favored and compromise is difficult; confrontation is not enjoyed and prepared counter proposals uncommon. This trying assignment for the bargainer would probably occur in

A. Buenos Aires

B. Nagasaki

C. Anchorage

10. Preparation by clearly identifying the issues of the pending negotiation is the dominant trait in these bargainers. They make their offers clearly and assertively and are confident and optimistic in expecting that such discipline to carry them through. They tolerate confrontation well, but

surprisingly are not prone to easy compromise. Such conduct might be witnessed in

   A. Berlin
   B. New Orleans
   C. Rio de Janeiro

11. These negotiators show considerable respect for the legalities of the transaction. Aggressive by nature they tend to stand confrontation well, haggle, and therefore are likely to have alternative positions ready. We would likely be in

   A. London
   B. Rome
   C. Los Angeles

12. Risk averseness is generally considered to be a handicap in those parties who participate in negotiating. While such a trait is frequently tied to the personality of a particular person, some cultures do not generally harbor such a trait. You would more likely to see this trait in

   A. Tokyo
   B. Seattle
   C. Moscow

See Answers page 208

The "Born Negotiator" Analysis

Score as follows

Question No. 1.	A-	15 points
	B-	7 points
	C-	11 points
Question No. 2.	A-	6 points
	B-	14 points
	C-	10 points
Question No. 3.	A-	13 points
	B-	5 points
	C-	9 points
Total Score:		_____ points

Training is easier and faster if the "trainee" possesses natural inclinations in the field of study. The practice of negotiation is certainly such a field, and success depends on highly disciplined behavior. This little test attempts to uncover a party's certain natural inclinations. Three negotiation situations were looked at, and the following scores suggest some conclusions about your nature and the practice of negotiations.

18 to 22 : Strong inclination to bargain effectively.

23 to 26 : Some resistance to hard bargaining but easily trainable.

27 to 34 : Easy going nature; not greatly.interested in negotiation.

35 to 42 : Uncomfortable with negotiation practices.

What personality traits, or mental sets, are likely to affect, or even determine, the likelihood of success in negotiation? The results observed by the authors in more than one hundred seminars involving mock negotiation, as well as the research and writing of students of the field, lend validity to these conclusions:

- A person who is more concerned with avoiding a loss (risk averse) than making a gain works at a disadvantage.
- Some persons cannot stand up against an aggressive or persistent opponent.
- Some persons have a need to be liked that is stronger than their need to win a negotiation for their company.
- Some persons feel that the negotiation process is degrading, that haggling is beneath them.
- Some persons are overly combative and cannot help antagonizing their opponents over minor, or even insignificant, points and are sure the are doing a good job thereby.

Persons whose mental set is largely the opposite of the above statements possess personality traits that are likely to lead to success in negotiation, given some training mixed with an apprentice period in the field.

Do You Agree With These Generalizations?

1. While parties having a credible belief that they can persuade others (A) make good negotiators it is not necessarily the key to effective negotiation. High aspirations, however, are essential and are particularly effective against a low aspirant (C).

2. There is a natural reluctance to being seen as "greedy" yet high initial demands do not seem to adversely affect a negotiation. It may be part of the psychology of lowering expectations which assists the other in crafting a good deal. Statement A is the incorrect one. The warning also is clear that concession behavior must be restrained; large concessions tend to foretell a loss (B).

3. The statement in A does not seem to be supported by experience. Apparently one's general skill does carry over sufficiently to mind reading. The old army strategist's saying is probably more appropriate when it advises "one cannot read the mind of the enemy but you should have a fair estimate of the enemy's capabilities." In regard to telephone negotiations Charlene may be the big winner that she thinks she is. Telephone negotiators usually favor the prepared which typically is initially the caller. There can be big winners here, and of course where there is a big winner there is sometimes a big loser (B). Bullheaded persons are not pleasant to be around, but they do populate negotiation tables. This unpopular trait, however, does not seem

to unduly impede those so inclined in bargaining sessions (C).

4. If statement A were only true? The reality is that most people and that includes negotiators, tend to assume that the other party has more advantages, more "chips" available for use in the session then they do. When a party has done his homework, the opposite supposition, i.e., "that you have more power," assists in carrying out your strategy. Statements B and C are true. Sadly, most negotiators who finish a tough session feel that they have done a good job. Reality sets in later for the loser when this party discovers certain aspects of the transaction and how others fared. Some pieces of business, i.e, tactics, come naturally to some people, and they may not even know their tactics have names.

How Well Do You Dance?
The Utility Schedule

If you selected any number but $9,000 in the exercise, you have contributed to the data social scientists have gathered regarding such behavior. Contrary to what one might expect to be common sense, academic theories offer that knowledge of the other party's utility schedule can upset one's own thinking. Because bargainers want to make a deal as quickly as possible they tend to aim for a marketable settlement. This means that the counteroffer is likely to be moderate and more reasonable than a proposal coming from a party ignorant of the other's thinking. There is a further reason for this behavior: many like to be thought of as fair and therefore attempt to accommodate to what they perceive to be the other's thinking. But, here's the rub: if the counteroffer comes in softer than the opponent expects, he or she will entertain a change in thinking and generate higher expectations, thus causing the formation of a new utility schedule. These theories have been borne out and replicated repeatedly in a wide variety of seminars and training sessions given by the authors.

Ignorance, then, can in some ways be "bliss." Therefore, unless the party knowing of the other's utility schedule can restrain its own thinking by carrying on in such a manner as to do nothing that will increase the expectations of the other. Uninformed bargainers tend to engage in longer negotiations but make fewer and smaller concessions which, after all, is the way to better settlements for them. And so, a common mental mistake is not uncommon here. Only the most disciplined can resist the temptation to try to "fit" their offer into the (presumed) mind-set of the other.

Thus, it has been asserted that knowledge of the opponent's utility schedule might cause bargainers to temper their own demands and hence actually "self sabotage" their position to some extent.

In practice, the above observations and conclusions sound a warning to the novice negotiator: do not be wrongly influenced by having secret information about the other party's utility schedule. Utility schedules are indeed fragile.

How Well Do You Practice Concessions? The Monetary Increment Game

A frequent mistake in bidding and counter offering is for the speaker to forget where the speaker has been or where the speaker is going. This is particularly true in the quantitative sense. In the heat of a session a party may be called on to move from a particular position. Assume that the $39,000 gambit won't fly, what should be the increased amount? Of course this decision is dependent on the many matters but the *percentage* of raise is important. The other party is consciously or unconsciously influenced by the degree to which this change occurs. A large percentage change from the previous bid must have a good reason—to the ears of the other side. Otherwise, that side may be getting the impression that the speaker was just "shooting from the hip," not the happiest of judgments in this serious business.

It is believed to be important that the other party not interpret a party's concession behavior in such a way that it leads to a rise in expectations. These expectations result in a changed objective and can lead to unsatisfactory negotiations, including a deadlock. Many sessions involve more than three counteroffers but the above illustrates the principle of proportionality.

For that reason it is generally recommended that erratic behavior, made by Bidder A here (moved up $4,500 then only $500), be avoided unless there is some other reason for the offering. The same can be said for Bidder C whose second concession is larger than the first. The behavior of Bidder B, here($3,000, then $2,000, attempts to send the message that one's concessions are narrowing, leading toward a logical point.

Can You Spot A Tactic?

1. The answer is Statement B. This is the "personalization" tactic. Simply, one uses personal not business reasons why a deal should be made or a concession given. Such an approach has no logic or ethics to support it. In the first place this is a business deal and the negotiator is an agent representing another; one's personal problems are neither proper nor relevant to the matter at hand. Ethically, there is risk in asking for personal help as such usually carries with it the implied promise of a returned favor in the future, a possibility which is not to one's principal's interest.

2. Laura may be exposed to the missing element (or person, document, etc) tactic, Statement A. When this behavior arises the victim must decide just what is going on. There are many possible reasons for the "missing" to remain so. It could be that the other side is negotiating with a competitor and using this as a backup plan; or they are not ready for a deal, or there is no budget approval for the commitment, or they are just trying to wear the other side down.

3. Statement C contains the clue. But the other possibilities are present and tie in with the concept of lowballing. When an unexpected favorable offer is made the offeree must be careful to look for the possibility that there is a reason which might do harm later. If the party is trying to "buy in" to the business, little injury is done. However, if the other side desperately needs the contract because of financial difficulties an offeree may be signing on to

trouble. Either the party will breach or, if not breach, threaten to breach and demand to renegotiate the deal. Or, even worse, the other contractor may have a post-contract strategy by which it knows how to take on "extras" (for which it charges) that the first party was not aware of. After all the other party usually knows more about his business that the stranger.

4. Statement B is meant here. The old salesperson technique of forcing closure is the "deadline" technique. "Only if you act today can you get this price," for example, has been with us forever. Yet, without some deadlines traffic would move slowly. It is important however for the party to recognize the possibility that a tactic is being used. Experienced bargainers, where appropriate, test these demands. "Oh, that's too bad, I can see we can't take advantage of this wonderful opportunity today; we would need three to four days to check this through our system," is one reply by which this aggressive move may be verified.

5. Statement B is intended here. Almost everyone has limited, or restricted, authority to some extent. It is an open question whether the practice of withholding power is an advantage or disadvantage in a particular case. There are anecdotes galore to show its value and its pitfalls. What is essential, however, is to recognize that it is a tactic, whether so intended or not. Rationales for its use vary. They may include reevaluating one's position, conferring with a specialist or expert, to have a further review of the facts and positions, looking for errors, examining the fine print, raising undefined issues, moving away from an untenable position, or even to say no politely.

6. The "transference" tactic is called by a number of names (monkey on the back, the bogey, etc.), but whatever the label the game is the same: one attempts to transfer one's

problem to the other negotiator. Statement B. The conduct is one of simply asking for help from your opponent. It feeds on his or her feeling of self-worth with the objective of making your problems their problems. It is considered a non-aggressive approach, generally judged ethical, and permits the other party to "show off." This technique has several risks, however. It can, for example, reveal the pleader's weaknesses, and even provide an opportunity for the other side to restructure the specifications to their advantage.

7. This behavior probably works best against the novice. Statement B identifies the concept. A good example is the consumer purchase of a new car. This is not a simple deal as the sellers well know. There is a dragging it out, suggesting good news, then "reluctantly" informing the buyer that the "manager" can't accept that offer but now offers a "restructured" offer. When a couple, for example, "invests" an entire Saturday with this "piece of business" somehow they think that they must make a deal or the whole unpleasant effort was wasted.

How Sensitive Are You To The Negotiator's Background?

1. Quito. If those who negotiate there follow the perceived Latin America mode the behavior described would fit.

2. Paris. The traditional French style follows the formal training in what is called the Cartesian method. They look for an outline of the agreement, following the practice of treaty-making over the centuries.

3. Stockholm. Scandinavians are generally perceived as well received in the world. They do not have a tradition of being loud talkers, are sociable and because of the liberal tendencies of these regions are highly flexible.

4. London. Hierarchy, or class, is a traditional way of behaving in England. The long history of the superior authority carries over in team assignments.

5. Chicago. Perception is everything and for good or bad the American is thought to be loud and fast talking and eager to get to the point.

6. Manchester. The English still harbor some resentment to being labeled "in trade." It is not that they are not good at it and are world wide traders, only that gentle persons do not, for example, seem to "haggle." They are not considered to be great on preparation for a negotiation.

7. Bogota. This describes the "Latin" temperament.

8. Riyadh. It is believed that those in the Middle East (here Saudi Arabia) depend a great deal on their measure of the prospective contractor. While details are important in the final agreement no consent will move forward unless these bargainers are satisfied that they are dealing with a dependable party.

9. Nagasaki. While more Western ways are being practiced in the Far East, the status of the parties is of great importance, as are the face saving features of a negotiation.

10. Berlin. Germans are tough negotiators, generally. They are know for preparation which unfortunately may not include great tolerance for compromise and alternative proposals.

11. Los Angeles. The American style of negotiating is aggressive, to the point, and with no reluctance to handle confrontation.

12. Tokyo. Risk averseness, while a handicap to many, does not seem to affect the ability of the Japanese to negotiate well. Their other traits, being silently aggressive in nature, doing careful preparation, and exhibiting patience compensate for their tendency to be risk averse.